For a Peaceful and Just World　Vol.II

To realize a World Without Nuclear Weapons
Peace and Security in East Asia

OGATA YASUO

Japan Press Service

Tokyo

Copyright,2019,by Ogata Yasuo

Published by Japan Press Service
25-6,Sendagaya 4-chome Shibuya-ku,
Tokyo 151-0051,Japan
Phone: +81-3-3423-2381
Fax: +81-3-3423-2383
URL:www.japan-press.co.jp
Email: info@japan-press.co.jp

Printed in Japan
October 2019

ISBN 978-4-88048-093-0

Table of Contents

Preface *7*

Chapter I The Way to Peace and Security in East Asia

1, For Peace and Stability of the Korean Peninsula *12*
   10th General Assembly of the ICAPP (International Conference of Asian Political Parties)
   October 24-26, 2018, Moscow, Russia

2, First Summit between the US and DPRK *16*
   26th Annual Conference of the Global Network (Global Network Against Weapons and Nuclear Power in Space)
   June 22-24, 2018, Oxford, UK

3, Japan-U.S. military Cooperation in the field of Space Technologies *22*
   The Global Network's 25th Annual Conference
   April 7-9, 2017, Huntsville Alabama, U.S.A.

4, Prospects for an East Asia Community *29*
   International Symposium for an East Asian Community organized by Japan Asia Africa Latin America Solidarity Committee (Japan AALA),
   May 24, 2015, United Nations University, Tokyo

5, Cooperation for Peace in Northeast Asia *43*
   International Conference on Peace and Space for Global Security and Human Development
   Gandhi Institute of Technical and Management Studies (GITAM University) , November 18-20, 2016, Visakhapatnam, India

6, Politics in Japan and Environment for Peace in Northeast Asia
.... *50*
4th World Socialism Forum by Chinese Academy of Social Sciences
October 30-31, 2013, Beijing, China

Chapter II World Peace and Elimination of Nuclear Weapons

1, Historical adoption of the Treaty on the Prohibition of Nuclear Weapons.. *64*
2017 World Conference against A and H Bombs
August 3, 2017, Hiroshima

2, Five major nuclear powers hostile to the Ban Treaty................. *67*
2018 World Conference against A and H Bombs
August 2, 2018, Hiroshima

3, Demanding to Conclude a Treaty bans and eliminates nuclear weapons *70*
2016 World Conference against A and H Bombs
August 3, 2016, Hiroshima

4, 70th anniversary of the atomic bombings of in Hiroshima and Nagasaki.. *74*
2015 World Conference against A and H Bombs
August 3, 2015, Hiroshima

Chapter III Social Development and socialism

1, Global Financial Crisis and Socialism
-In the light of the world structural change- *80*
International Forum in Southwest Univ.
October 26-27, 2009, Chongqing, China

2, Paying High Regard to Specificity and Internal Logic of Social Development... *85*
    6th World Socialism Forum by Chinese Academy of Social Sciences
    October 16, 2015, Beijing, China

3, "The Belt and Road Project" and Regional Cooperation............ *91*
    The ICAPP Special Conference on "Rebuilding the Silk Road"
    October 14-16, 2015, Beijing, China

Chapter Ⅳ   Environment Preservation, Nuclear disaster & Human Trafficking

1, Experience and Lessons of Japan's Environmental Pollution of the Past 50 Years *98*
    The ICAPP Special Conference on "Promoting Green Development and Building a Beautiful Asia Together"
    May 29-31, 2013, Xi'an, China

2, For enhanced international cooperation in disaster response
.... *104*
    ICAPP Special Conference on Natural Disasters & Environmental Protection
    March 2-4, 2015, Putrajaya, Malaysia

3, Human Trafficking Today.. *110*
    3rd ICAPP Workshop on Human Trafficking
    March 12, 2016, Islamabad, Pakistan

ChapterⅤ   Mahatma Gandhi & Social Development

Mahatma Gandhi and Japan
-An Approach towards East Asian Peace- *120*
    The International Conference on Gandhi, Disarmament and Development
    October 4-6, 2013, Indore, Madhya Pradesh, India

Preface

Since the publication of my pamphlet "JCP Speaks for a Peaceful and Just World" in 2013, which contained the text of speeches I made, I had a lot of great opportunities to attend a variety of international conferences, seminars and fora (nearly 30 times during 6 years) such as the International Conference of Asian Political Parties (ICAPP), the Global Network Against Weapons and Nuclear Power in Space, the World Conference against A and H Bombs, and various university-hosted symposia. I made those speeches on behalf of the Japanese Communist Party and as co-chair of the World Conference against A and H Bombs. I selected for this pamphlet nearly 20 speeches I made at those international meetings.

Looking back on the past six years, I have a strong impression that, indeed, the world has been changing very rapidly in positive as well as in negative ways. The real world offers such a complex reality and we must analyse real world events and phenomena scientifically and objectively. When a negative change prevails for a while, we should admit this reality in the political culture, maybe acknowledging with a "C'est la vie". However, in the face of difficult circumstances, I become filled with a fighting spirit and increased awareness of the need to take action.

After the inauguration of the Trump Administration in the U.S., the phenomenon of right-wing populism has reared its ugly head in the world. In particular, we see that the extreme right-wing forces are advancing in a number of parliaments with their blatant racism and hatred against immigrants and minorities in the society. This extremist tendency also marginalizes or even intimidates some of the left forces to some extent.

We have also another challenge and that is to fight back against the extremism which claims to represent Islam and is associated with spreading terrorism throughout the world. We can never accept this as representative of the Islamic faith.

The rise of China, both economically and politically, has been pronounced during those six years. It is incumbent for us to observe carefully U.S.-China relations and recognize them as big power interactions. In China, unfortunately, excessive focus on nationalism is increasing at the popular level. It seems to me that neither the Chinese Communist Party nor the Government of China have taken on the responsibility to control and suppress such an extreme nationalism. As a result, China has now manifested a kind of hegemonism and big-power chauvinism in certain fields of in the international arena. This negative tendency has prevented China from gaining the trust and respect of the peoples of the region and the world, and achieving its growth and development goals.

We have watched the steady development in the small and medium-sized countries that have been good drivers in the international political arena which I touch upon in this pamphlet.

While nearly 75 years have passed since the end of the World War II, we still have very important challenges to confront in Japan such as the need to fight back the ultranationalist form of historical revisionism which glorifies the war of aggression in Asia caused by Japanese militarism. In this sense, a true postwar era has not yet come about and we must continue to work to overcome the resurfacing of the ultra nationalism and its desire to rewrite the history of Japan and Asia.

This pamphlet covers a wide range of issues such as peace and security in East Asia; dangers associated with the strengthened Japan-U.S. military cooperation in every field including outer space; world peace and the elimination of nuclear weapons; the global financial crisis and socialism; environment preservation, nuclear disaster; human trafficking; and Mahatma Gandhi and his achievements. All texts remain as they were originally published.

Preface

I sincerely hope that these texts will assist you in obtaining a better understanding of the JCP policy and positions on the issues discussed.

September 2019

OGATA Yasuo

Chapter I

The Way to Peace and Security in East Asia

1, For Peace and Stability of the Korean Peninsula

10th General Assembly of the ICAPP (International Conference of Asian Political Parties)
October 24-26, 2018, Moscow, Russia

Honorable Chairpersons,
Dear friends,

I welcome the fact that the 10th General Assembly of the International Conference of Asian Political Parties (ICAPP) is being held in Moscow under the theme of meeting the needs of the times, and express my gratitude to the organizers – United Russia and the Secretariat of the ICAPP.

How to build peace and cooperation in Asia is a major challenge that the ICAPP has consistently addressed since its founding. First of all, I welcome the recent dramatic and powerful change for peace that is taking place in Northeast Asia.

Until last year, the Korean Peninsula experienced extremely high tensions and it was feared that an accidental clash might trigger a war or even a nuclear war. But this year, the leaders of the two Koreas held summit meetings three times, and the heads of North Korea and the United States also held a summit for the first time ever. In those meetings, they agreed to promote the denuclearization of the Korean Peninsula and the building of a peace structure, and the situation has dramatically changed from hostility to working for a resolution of issues through dialogue. As a political party persistently calling for a peaceful and diplomatic resolution of the dispute, the Japanese Communist Party heartily welcomes and strongly supports this new move to establish a lasting peace.

In April this year, the JCP made a request to the countries concerned regarding the following two points: along with efforts to denuclearize the Korean Peninsula, it is essential to build a structure promoting peace in an integrated and comprehensive manner in order to ease tensions and improve relations between the two Koreas and between North Korea and the United States; and to negotiate measures to overcome deep distrust and to build trust between the US and North Korea, and implement them step by step. As of now, Pyongyang has presented some concrete measures for denuclearization, and Washington has also shown its intent to take corresponding measures. We believe it is important to promote this process based on the spirit of "quid pro quo".

This move toward peace has been supported not only by the relevant countries but also by strong international opinion and global public campaigns opposing war. In order to achieve this road map to bring peace to the Korean Peninsula, it is necessary for political parties as well as national governments to actively campaign to reach this goal.

The normalization of diplomatic ties between Japan and North Korea is another essential element in establishing peace on the Korean Peninsula. The foundation for normalization is the Japan-North Korea Pyongyang Declaration signed in 2002. It is particularly vital for Japan to express deep remorse for its past colonization of the Peninsula, as a first step toward normalization.

In addition, the JCP calls for creating a multilateral framework for peace and stability in Northeast Asia. At the JCP Congress five years ago, we proposed the Initiative for Peace and Cooperation in Northeast Asia. This initiative calls for concluding a Northeast-Asian version of the Treaty of Amity and Cooperation in Southeast Asia (TAC) and requiring signatories to resolve any dispute through dialogue. We are also certain that the Six-Party Talks on the North Korea issue, as represented by its joint statement in 2005, can be used to create the framework for peace and stability in Northeast Asia.

The current moves working to establish peace in Northeast Asia will lead to establishing a lasting peace throughout East Asia. The provisions of the TAC correspond to the principles of the Bali Declaration, which was adopted in 2011 at the East Asia Summit attended by 18 nations, including 10 ASEAN members along with China, India, Russia, and the US. It is feasible to upgrade the declaration to a treaty. Let's work together to bring success to the peace process on the Korean Peninsula and achieve peace in Northeast Asia, with a vision for establishing a lasting peace throughout East Asia, South Asia, and Southeast Asia.

Another topic I want to discuss is the move to abolish nuclear weapons, which has been at the core of the North Korea crisis. In 2016, the UN General Assembly confirmed the necessity to build a legal framework to ban nuclear weapons, the most inhumane weapons of mass destruction, following the Biological Weapons Convention (BWC) and the Chemical Weapons Convention (CWC). In July 2017, the Treaty on the Prohibition of Nuclear Weapons was approved by a vote of 122 UN member states in favor. So far, 69 nations have signed the treaty and 19 have ratified it.

This historic treaty states as follows: "Deeply concerned about the catastrophic humanitarian consequences that would result from any use of nuclear weapons, and recognizing the consequent need to completely eliminate such weapons, which remains the only way to guarantee that nuclear weapons are never used again under any circumstances". Far from being incompatible with the 191-member NPT, this treaty complements the NPT and generates a hard-to-stop momentum for peace.

Nuclear-weapons-free-zone treaties have been concluded in various parts of the world, and currently cover 114 countries. Among them are ASEAN nations, Mongolia, and countries in Central Asia and the South Pacific. This fact is also reflected in the adoption of the nuclear weapons ban treaty.

The nuclear weapons ban treaty specifies the important role of parliamentarians as well. The ICAPP has repeatedly called for realizing a world free of nuclear weapons. Its Phnom Penh Declaration adopted in 2010 expressed support for "negotiations on a nuclear weapons convention", and the Colombo Declaration in 2014 called on the international community to promptly launch such talks. The treaty will take effect if 50 countries ratify it. As a political party of the only atomic-bombed nation in the world, the JCP calls on all the participants and friends to work together to have the convention come into force as early as possible.

Lastly, I would like to note that it is important for us to cooperate on common issues of promoting peace and social progress by going beyond differences in thought and beliefs, and work on our national governments together. A platform to achieve this is the ICAPP – a unique organization where political parties from all over the world have the opportunity to meet in order to discuss issues together. I would like to conclude my speech by calling for further joint efforts to enhance the role of the ICAPP. Thank you for your kind attention.

2, First Summit between the US and DPRK

26th Annual Conference of the Global Network (Global Network Against Weapons and Nuclear Power in Space)
June 22-24, 2018, Oxford, UK

I would like to express my sincere gratitude for the invitation to the Global Network's 26th Annual Conference at Oxford. Taking advantage of this occasion, I am very much pleased to participate in the event to protest at the major US, NATO Military space communications and control center nearby Croughton Air Force Base. I remember a series of huge demonstrations at the beginning of 1980's against deployments of INF (Intermediate-range nuclear force) in UK as well as throughout Western Europe.

At that time, as I was a reporter of the Japanese newspaper "Akahata" based in Paris, I visited frequently Greenham Common and other places in UK and reported the various activities, especially impressed by Women's Camp. I am very happy to witness great activities going on continuously.

I will focus my talk on two great events which are developing in the international arena since the last conference, that is, the adoption of the UN treaty on the prohibition of nuclear weapons last July and dramatic change of the situation in Korean Peninsula to which I referred as severe military confrontations between the US and North Korea in my presentation of the last conference.

Firstly, the adoption of the treaty which explicitly prohibits nuclear weapons is a historic achievement made by the many years of collective efforts by Hibakusha, civil society groups and organizations from around the world, and the many governments seeking to realize a world without nuclear weapons. I was very much honored sharing the explosion of enthusiasm at the moment of the adoption on the spot.

Chapter1 The Way to Peace and Security in East Asia

ICAN received the Nobel Peace Prize in 2017. We heartily welcome and congratulate the laureate, recognizing, as people say, this is the great encouragement to the movements and public opinions demanding abolition of nuclear weapons for long years.
The ratification process is now open to all the countries, in spite of increasing pressure against it by nuclear powers such as US, Russia, France, UK and China, forming common front called P5 Group. Up to now, 59 countries have signed the treaty and 10 countries have ratified it.

What is very important is to accelerate this process because we need at least 50 nations to ratify the treaty to get it into force. For that, let's strengthen our campaigns by all peoples and all governments of the world, including backward-looking nations to this treaty. It is more and more clear that the only guarantee against the spread and use of nuclear weapons is to eliminate them without delay.

As the inclusion of nuclear weapons states in the treaty process is vital in order to realize the total elimination of nuclear weapons, the treaty leaves the door wide open for their participation. For that, the treaty also establishes a framework for them. It stipulates two options for their accession in the treaty; 1) destroy nuclear weapons first, then join the treaty; 2) join the treaty first, then destroy them as soon as possible.

We have launched the International Hibakusha Signature Collection Campaign since April 2016, which aims to collect hundreds of millions of signatures around the world in support of the total elimination of nuclear weapons. We have collected more than 3 million signatures. On the first day of the UN Conference for the treaty negotiations in New York, we submitted to Chairperson Ellen White and the UN Secretariat big mountains of signatures in front of the UN Headquarters. We believe that this is indeed one of the most important factors pushing for our common achievement.

We have decided to continue this Signature Collection Campaign,

17

attaching more importance to it since the adoption of the Treaty. I would like to sincerely call for your signature and your expanded cooperation by making the best use of new situation of the adoption of this historic treaty as well as the completely new situation around the Korean Peninsula.

We now concentrate on our efforts to change the attitude of the Japanese government that has expressed opposition to signing the treaty, reiterating that the U.S. nuclear deterrence is essential under the Japan-U.S. alliance.

They assert that Japan's signing onto the treaty would damage the legitimacy of the deterrence strategy. They hold the nuclear deterrence theory as a reason to oppose the treaty. That is an idea that would allow nations to resort to using nuclear weapons in the event of security-related emergency even though it would bring about a great human tragedy similar to ones experienced in Hiroshima and Nagasaki.

We have launched a public campaign to demand the Japanese government to sign the treaty, otherwise, to change the government itself in favor of the treaty.

Next, I would like to refer to the summit between the US President Donald Trump and DPRK Chairman Kim Jong Un that was held 10 days ago with great success after successful holding of the inter-Korean summit at the end of April. Both summits have contributed tremendously to peace and stability of the Korean Peninsula and a peaceful solution of North Korea's nuclear and missile issue through diplomatic means. They are literally historic events that are going to end the last and remained confrontation between the East and the West.

It is indeed for the first time that leaders of the US and North Korea together with South Korea are sharing fundamentally the common direction to evade war, cease hostility and seek confidence-building.
In addition, what is new in the US side is that the CIA and the Pentagon have become important actors for negotiations and dialogue, both of

which usually played a role in favor of military solutions. In this sense, I must look with compound eyes to the policies of President Trump as we have strong criticism in many areas against his security policies.

The denuclearization of the Korean Peninsula could not take place in a single stroke. It would take rather some time at least. In this sense, it is only a beginning of the process which needs close collaborations among the concerned countries and the international community.

Negotiations have been done and will continue in order to complete the denuclearization of the Korean Peninsula and the building of a permanent peace structure in Northeast Asia, by implementing an integrated approach, sharing goals in a timely fashion, with the principle of "commitment for commitment, action for action".

It will be more and more important to utilize peace frameworks in Northeast Asia that endorse and promote this process, such as a resumption of the 6-Party talks which existed before or newly holding of regional conferences or fora. We have made a proposal for peace and cooperation in Northeast Asia, especially to conclude a Treaty of Amity and Cooperation in this region as rules for peace by which member countries need to abide, including renunciation of the use of force, peaceful resolution of conflicts, non-interference in internal affairs, and promotion of effective dialogues and cooperation for confidence-building.

I must point out the anecdotal attitude of the Japanese Government that has still insisted on possible military measures, continuing maximum pressure against North Korea and negative attitude to dialogues and negotiations. At the same time, Mr. Abe is following Mr. Trump, saying "Japan is always 100% together with the US". It is the symbolic stance of Japan, completely subordinate to the US.

For the peace and stability of the Korean peninsula, both inter-Korean and US-North Korea sound and good relationships are essential.

Both are going on very well. At the same time, the improvement of Japan-North Korea relationship is indispensable. We sincerely wish that the Japanese Government will change the negative attitude to dialogue, following good example of President Trump and will have chance to realize direct contacts with them on the basis of the Japanese-North Korean Pyongyang declaration in 2002.

I would like to underline that using North Korea's nuclear and missile development as a flimsy pretext, the Abe administration has gone ahead with the introduction of a state-of-the-art BMD system. The Japanese government appears to be intent on the introduction of THAAD missiles and the deployment of Aegis Ashore, a land-based component of the Aegis BMD system.

In order to build the capability to attack enemy bases, the Japanese Government has declared to have a plan to introduce long–range cruise missiles, stealth jet fighters F35B, aircraft carriers and so on.

After setting up a joint working group on military cooperation in space on the basis of the 2015 guidelines for Japan-U.S. defense cooperation, which described space-related plans for the first time. The Japanese Government is preparing to establish a special military command of cyber and space by 2020. This is aimed not only at improving military and intelligence gathering capabilities, but also at waging wars together with the US even in the space.

For that, the military budget for space will expand 3 or 5 times more in 3 years, reaching the order of 200 billion yen (1.8 billion dollars) by buying more and more military machines from the US, following Trump's policy "buy Americans". Now, the US government is becoming No.1 partner for the contracts of military trade.

Finally, two great events to which I referred, the adoption of the treaty and the new dynamism in the Korean Peninsula, are vitally essential to fight back the reactionary offensives and military expansions and to strengthen the ongoing struggles against the construction of new base in Okinawa and other bases for U.S. missile defense in Japan. We are determined to open a new perspective in Japan as well as in the region for safety and new development. Thank you for your attention.

3, Japan-U.S. military Cooperation in the field of Space Technologies

The Global Network's 25th Annual Conference
April 7-9, 2017, Huntsville Alabama, U.S.A.

I'd like to express my gratitude for the invitation to participate in the Global Network's 25th annual conference and for being given the opportunity to speak. As Huntsville is the manufacturing site for missile systems and the home of the Redstone Arsenal and the Space Command's directorate for 'missile defense' and with the danger of a space-based arms race growing, it is highly significant to hold the conference in this city to oppose missile defense systems and the expansion of military use of outer space.

I'll focus my presentation on the increasingly dangerous situations in Northeast Asia, the advances in North Korea's nuclear weapons and missile program, and the U.S. Trump administration's responses to the North Korea issue.

North Korea conducted two nuclear tests and launched more than 20 missiles in 2016. On March 6 this year, it fired four ballistic missiles that landed in the Sea of Japan after reaching an altitude of 260 kilometers. Regarding this missile launch, North Korea made the unprecedented announcement stating "the exercise was held by military units tasked to attack U.S. bases in Japan." Following this announcement, Japan, the United States, and South Korea conducted a joint ballistic missile defense exercise for two days from March 14 in the waters near Japan and South Korea. And very recently again, North Korea fired a newly developed ballistic missile just before the first US-China summit.

Regarding relations with North Korea, the Trump administration criticized its predecessor's policy of "strategic patience" as a failed policy and began arguing for a confrontational approach toward North Korea which places "all options are on the table", implicitly including a military option.

It was reported that the February meeting between President Trump and Prime Minister Abe confirmed that all options include a U.S. military attack on North Korea in response to moves to conduct a ballistic missile launch test.

When U.S. Foreign Secretary Tillerson visited Japan and South Korea in mid-March, he announced that Washington will take a "new approach" to the North Korean threat which "includes the military option".

The United States was at the brink of carrying out a preemptive military attack against North Korea in 1994. This military crisis was averted through direct communications between Washington and Pyongyang, in addition to strong opposition from China, resistance to a military option by South Korea, and Japan's hesitation to support the use of military force. At present, it is clearly understood by all parties that a military strike would cause catastrophic damage with devastating consequences, making it difficult for the U.S. to implement the military option.

Given the current deadlock over measures to stop North Korea's tests, it is difficult to ignore the possibility of a preemptive attack against the North. If such action is taken, North Korea might attempt to launch its ballistic missiles in retaliation. The current situation of escalating tensions is prompting both South Korea and Japan to improve their defenses system to intercept missiles launched from the North. A state-of-the-art missile defense system placed in South Korea and Japan would become a new risk factor in the region and public awareness of the increasingly tense situation in Northeast Asia must be raised.

Using North Korea's nuclear and missile development programs as a pretext, the Japanese government is rapidly going ahead with the introduction of a state-of-the-art BMD system. The focus of this move is to develop a ballistic missile intercept system jointly with the U.S. and to strengthen Japan's readiness to respond.

The Japanese Defense Ministry has decided on measures to achieve this. They plan to complete the Japan-U.S. joint development of SM-3 Block IIA interceptors designed for Aegis warships by the end of fiscal 2017 and begin to deploy them to vessels of the Maritime Self-Defense Force in fiscal 2020. The ministry also has a plan to procure PAC-3 MSE interceptors and deploy them to the Air SDF in 2019, a year ahead of schedule.

In addition, the defense authorities intend to introduce the Terminal High Altitude Area Defense (THAAD) anti-missile system earlier than scheduled. They originally planned to put THAAD missiles in place after the current five-year defense build-up program comes to an end in 2018, but the government appropriated 33.1 billion yen (280 million dollar) for research and development costs in the third supplementary budget for fiscal 2016.

When the Japanese defense minister visited Guam in January to inspect the THAAD interceptors deployed at the U.S. Andersen Air Force Base, she expressed her intent to take into consideration the introduction of a THAAD system as one of the measures to enhance Japan's missile defense capability.

In February, the ruling Liberal Democratic Party set up a task force to discuss how to enhance the BMD system and the capability to attack enemy bases.

The Japanese government appears to be intent on the introduction of THAAD missiles and the deployment of Aegis Ashore, a land-based component of the Aegis BMD system. We have to face the fact that under the Abe-Trump alliance recently formed, the two governments are accelerating cooperation in this field.

In addition, the Japanese government's move to strengthen the BMD system also matches the Trump administration's "Buy American" policy as Aegis Ashore and THAAD are products of Lockheed Martin. Taking advantage of Japan's relaxed rules on arms exports, Prime Minister Abe is expanding Japan-U.S. technical and economic cooperation to the military field in order to support President Trump politically and economically.

Since Prime Minister Abe took power in 2012, the government has been promoting Japan-U.S. military cooperation in the field of space technologies. PM Abe in the summit meeting with President Obama in 2013 agreed to accept the placement of an additional U.S. X-band radar facility to detect missile launches. In 2014, an X-band radar base was constructed and started operations at Kyogamisaki in northern Kyoto. This is the second X-band radar base in Japan after the one placed in Aomori's Tsugaru City.

The 2015 guidelines for Japan-U.S. defense cooperation include space-related plans for the first time ever. The Japanese Self-Defense Forces and the U.S. Forces set up a joint working group on cooperation in this regard.

The Abe government in 2015 decided on its third basic plan for space policies. The top priority of the plan's three targets is to secure Japan's use of space for security purposes. This is aimed at improving military and intelligence gathering capabilities. The basic plan takes on an obvious military flavor. It proposes to strengthen the Japan-U.S. alliance through increased cooperation in the development and deployment of space technologies, with Japan's previous peaceful use of space policy being taken over by the space for defense policy. Japan is becoming more and more involved in the U.S.-led missile defense initiative.

The Diet Resolution on the Peaceful Utilization of Space of 1969, based on the pacifist constitution, restricted space development and utilization only to peaceful purposes and prohibited its utilization for the military.

Nevertheless, the Fundamental Law Concerning Space of 2008 positioned the space development and utilization as an activity contributing to the security of the country, thus paving the way for its utilization for the military.

The Japanese Constitution prohibits the exercise of the right of collective self-defense and all the past LDP governments have continued to adhere to this position. However, in 2015, the Abe cabinet railroaded "the national security legislation" through the national Diet, enabling Japan to exercise the right to collective self-defense in order to participate in wars waged by the United States anywhere in the world.

The U.S. armed forces are geared to conduct military operations in Northeast Asia with the support of Japanese military capabilities. If Japan participates in a U.S. missile defense action, Japan will be forced to exercise the right to collective self-defense. "The national security legislation" was essential to enable the government of Japan not only to fight wars together with the United States on the earth, but also in space. I emphasize that Japan is becoming a country which can fight wars together with the United States even in space under the pretext of protecting Japan's peace and security.

Missile development is to missile defense what a pike is to a shield. Both missile development and missile defense will bring about an arms race and only lead to raising tensions among nations, resulting in the creation of military predominance and preemptive attack arrangements. They will not defend people's security at all and will require a huge amount of taxpayer's money. They will worsen relations with neighboring countries and will become a source of tensions in the end. As we are witnessing strong opposition from China and Russia to the U.S. deployment of THAAD in South Korea, advancement of missile defense will bring about a heightening of tensions in the region. In this regard, the Abe Administration contains dangerous elements of Japan's past militarism because far from expressing remorse for Japan's past wars of aggression, it embraces the ideology of eulogizing the wars as "wars of justice".

The only way to address and resolve the issues threatening peace in Northeast Asia through dialogue. There is no platform for talks among the states concerned in Northeast Asia. There is no stable route to dialogue between the United States and North Korea. In the past, the Six Party Talks worked, and in 2005, all parties agreed on an epoch-making road map for normalizing relationships between the United States and North Korea, between Japan and North Korea, and creating peace in Northeast Asia. However difficult it may be, we have to return to this map to try to solve the problems through diplomacy.

I would like to emphasize that military means to resolve any issues are likely to bring us all to ruin. After the crisis that erupted on the Korean Peninsula in 1994, William Perry recommended in his report that they should address the crisis with the understanding that the premise that the current regime of North Korea would last for the time being, and thus they should avoid giving priority to military options, and they should approach the issues at hand in a comprehensive and integrated manner through peaceful means and negotiations. These recommendations are valid to this day.

In conclusion, I would like to mention the ongoing struggles against the construction of bases for U.S. missile defense in Japan. Residents of Kyoto and Aomori are opposing the installation of X-band radar sites. It is important to inform citizens that missile defense can defend neither the land nor the citizens, will lead to ruin, and cost a fortune. Since the government is using scare tactics on Japanese citizens by greatly exaggerating the threat of attack by North Korea, they don't understand the real danger behind Japan's ongoing militarization. We are engaged in activities to inform as many citizens as possible about the inherent dangers of an arms race in space.

There are at present more than a hundred U.S. bases and facilities in Japan. Residents throughout Japan are firmly and continuously struggling for their removal. Okinawans are struggling against the construction of a new U.S. Marine Corps base in Nago City, the construction of U.S. Osprey helipads in Higashi Village, and the construction of F35 fighter pads on Iejima Island, Okinawans have created the "All Okinawans vs. the government" framework for struggle. This is a model similar to the joint struggles among opposition parties working together with citizens' movements opposing the government.

In the mainland of Japan, the Ronald Reagan, a nuclear-powered aircraft carrier, was deployed at the Yokosuka base near Tokyo, and state-of-the-art Aegis-equipped combat vessels have been deployed there. The Iwakuni Marine Corps base in Yamaguchi Prefecture and the Sasebo Naval base in Nagasaki Prefecture are being enhanced. Thus, U.S. bases in Japan are being upgraded to become major strongholds of the U.S. Marine Corps and U.S. carrier strike group for their mission to "rapidly deploy" worldwide.

People are persistently and continuously struggling for the withdrawal of the U.S. bases in Japan. For instance, they use legal action to document the sufferings caused by the bases, mobilize the general public for support, and sue for damages. Struggles today require that they should be globally integrated. Informing each other of our activities and strengthening our solidarity in transborder alliances, we will carry on the struggles opposing militarization and war.

4, Prospects for an East Asia Community

International Symposium for an East Asian Community organized by Japan Asia Africa Latin America Solidarity Committee (Japan AALA), May 24, 2015, United Nations University, Tokyo

When we observe the state of international relations in East Asia, we quickly notice a contrast between Southeast nations and Northeast nations. Southeast Asia has the framework of ASEAN (Association of Southeast Asian Nations) in place which has matured over the years into an integrated regional community. The ASEAN Community will come into being by the end of this year based on agreements related to cultural, social, economic, political, and security concerns. Northeast Asia has no such framework in place and is facing a number of challenges.

However, we can find some positive steps being taken in community building efforts across East Asia if we closely examine growing regional trends from a broad perspective.

One such attempt is seen with the formation of the East Asia Summit (EAS), which could possibly provide an integrative framework for the region. The EAS has held annual meetings since 2005, discussing issues related to the peaceful solution of conflicts and the mutually acceptable management of diverse economic interests. The summary documents that have emerged from the meetings can be seen as part of the initial preparation in application of the formation of a future East Asia community, though there is still a long way to go.

A, Importance of East Asia in a Structurally Changing World

1, Shift of Economic Power Balance

The center of gravity of the global economy is shifting to the Global South. According to the IMF, the total GDP of 34 OECD member states, which once had enjoyed nearly 60% of the world GDP in 2000, was surpassed by the total GDP of 150 developing countries in 2010 based on the purchase power parity (PPP). The GDP of the developing countries is projected to share 56% of the world GDP in 2017. The gap between the two clusters is expected to continue to wide.

The economic rise of the so-called emerging economies has been mainly driven by the rise of East Asian countries which has accelerated the shift of the global economic weight to Asia. The IMF World Economic Outlook, published in October 2014, projected that the total GDP of 7 emerging economies, including China and Indonesia, would amount to 3.78 trillion dollars on a PPP basis, exceeding the total GDP of the advanced G-7 economies, which is estimated to amount to 3.45 trillion dollars. China, which has become increasingly influential in East Asia, is projected to have a GDP of 1.76 trillion dollars, finally surpassing the projected U.S. GDP of 1.74 trillion.

The year 2015 may become the tipping point of the economic power balance between the North and the South (advanced economies vs. emerging economies) as well as between the East and the West (Asia vs. the Western nations). Joseph E. Stiglitz, a well-known economist, pointed out, "2014 was the last year in which the United States could claim to be the world's largest economic power. China enters 2015 in the top position, where it will likely remain for a very long time"[1].

The economic power shift has had its influence felt in the realm of international politics, resulting in more active roles played by developing countries calling for national sovereignty and peace. East Asian nations have been increasing their influence in the global political arena as well as in the global economy.

I include the U.S. when I consider possible multilateral frameworks in Northeast Asia and East Asia. The U.S. regional strategy of the so-called "Rebalance to Asia" is one of the most important factors to be

---

[1] Joseph E. Stiglitz, "The Chinese Century", *Vanity Fair* (January 2015)

taken into account when considering the topic of regional stability with its military and political/economic alliances and its relations with China.

2, Regional Achievement led by ASEAN

The 48 years of ASEAN's history is important in exploring of possibility of creating an East Asian Community. The ASEAN has transformed the once war-torn region into a community of peace while preserving a remarkable diversity in political systems, religions, and ethnic composition. It has blazed the trail by agreeing to mutually respect differences. Its principle is inclusiveness and its decisions are made by consensus.

ASEAN's experience provides realistic prospects for the establishment of an East Asian Community. The ASEAN has taken a series of initiatives to promote further regional integration. The establishment of ASEAN plus 3 (Japan, China and South Korea) is significant in that it may provide a possible basic framework for a more inclusive regional community.

The EAS is remarkable when viewed in this context. The annual EAS meetings are attended by representatives from eight countries outside the ASEAN, including three permanent members of the U.N. Security Council (China, Russia and the U.S.) as well as Japan and South Korea. While meetings are held by other regional communities such as the European Union (EU), the Community of Latin American and Caribbean States (CELAC) and the African Union (AU), there is no comparable regional summit meeting like the EAS with its attendance by the leaders of the major powers. The U.S. clearly attaches importance to the EAS when it states, "We're not only rebalancing towards Asia, we're also rebalancing our efforts within Asia" by putting the ASEAN at its core.

No country perceives the ASEAN as a threat. The ASEAN has made clear that all initiatives it takes should be ASEAN-centered, saying: ASEAN is in the driver's seat. EAS member states recognize and share international norms based on the U.N. Charter and other international laws. Such norms must be respected by all members including the major powers.

Any nation that is to join the EAS is required to ratify the Treaty of Amity and Cooperation in Southeast Asia (TAC). Article 10 of the treaty states, "[Each member state] shall not in any manner or form participate in any activity which shall constitute a threat" to another.

The extended TAC is to regulate relations between the ASEAN and outside member states. The treaty has three basic precepts as norms for peace and confidence-building: the TAC should be open and have no hypothetical enemy; security should be based on dialogue, confidence-building and peaceful solution of conflicts, not on heavy reliance on military deterrence; and nations should develop and cooperate with mutual respect while preserving diversity.

The EAS framework clearly has the potential to contribute to forming a future East Asian community. The 2011 EAS adopted the Declaration on the Principles for Mutually Beneficial Relations, putting importance on: non-interference in the internal affairs of another country; renunciation of the threat of use of force or use of force against another state; and settlement of differences and disputes by peaceful means. Although the declaration is not legally binding, it is morally binding among the members. Such principles as stated in the declaration could be the core elements for the security arrangements of a future broader community.

As the ASEAN becomes the community of Southeast Asia, taking a series of initiatives for peace and integration in East Asia, I hope to see the lessons learned from the ASEAN example adopted in Northeast Asia.

B, Possible Framework in Northeast Asia

1, Where We Stand

Northeast Asia is presently troubled with tension and instability.

Among the major factors contributing to this tension are the issue of North Korea which self-proclaims a nuclear weapons state, the territorial disputes in the East China Sea, and the enhanced U.S. military presence with the realignment of forward-deployed forces. Obviously, Japan's controversial interpretation of the wartime history is also a contentious issue as this year marks the 70th anniversary of the end of World War II.

Nevertheless, the prospect in Northeast Asia is not as dismal as it was in the late 1960's in Southeast Asia. The ASEAN was established in 1967. At that time, the region was torn by the Vietnam War while Thailand and Philippines, original members of the organization, provided military bases for the U.S.

Now, Northeast Asia already shares some experience in working together for peaceful settlement of disputes: the Six Party framework for negotiations on the North Korea nuclear issue. Although the framework is stalled for the time being, it worked for at least 5 years. The discussion went beyond the denuclearization of the Korean Peninsula. In September 2005, the parties issued a joint statement agreeing "to explore ways and means for promoting security cooperation in Northeast Asia". In February 2007, the parties also agreed on the establishment of five working groups, including one for the "Northeast Asia Peace and Security Mechanism", in order to carry out initial actions for the implementation of the joint statement. They even discussed the possibility of a regional multilateral mechanism and coming up with guiding principles for peace and security of the region. I believe a restart of the Six Party Talks framework is certainly in the realm of possibility.

Another initiative has also been proposed: a new treaty of friendship and cooperation encompassing the Indo-Pacific region to create a regional community across regions, including Northeast Asia. Indonesia presented this idea in May, 2013.

2, Challenges
China-U.S. Relations

One of interesting factors to predict dynamics of Northeast Asia is the U.S. - China relations. As the world is witnessing U.S. influence decreasing while China's influence is growing, this new global structural change is particularly noticeable in the bilateral relations between the two countries, whether you call it "the new relations of major powers" or not. The U.S. has embraced a strategy of "integrate but hedge" vis-à-vis China, aiming to cooperate in the pursuit of common interests while managing differences[2]. This is in sharp contrast to the past explicitly hostile U.S. strategy toward the former Soviet Union. We are now entering an era where there can be no war between the U.S. and China.

China's rise raises doubts regarding the long-term feasibility of U.S. policy to integrate China into the U.S-led global architecture. China has taken the initiative to establish the Asia Infrastructure Investment Bank (AIIB). This move is clearly the emergence of a new major player in the global economy because the proposed AIIB is not part of the existing U.S.-led global financial regime which includes the World Bank and the Asian Development Bank. The U.S. administration tried to persuade its allies and partners to stay out of the bank, yet the U.K, Germany and France expressed their willingness to be founding members in the bank, followed by Australia and South Korea. This new trend to offer an alternative to the U.S.-led system is growing against a backdrop of the unleashing economic potential of Asia and the funding of a series of mega-projects by China.

China has proposed a variety of economic initiatives. It includes the Silk Road Economic Zone Initiative[3] and the New Development Bank (formerly referred as the BRICS Development Bank with starting capital of 50 billion dollars) as well as the BRICS Reserve Fund of 100 billion dollars. China has also signed a 30-year-long 400-billion-dollar contract with Russia for natural gas which is the first major yuan-de-

---

2 A policy to integrate China into the existing U.S.-led international system as a responsible stakeholder while hedging against irresponsible behavior by China using a wide variety of measures including military deterrence.

3 A 400-billion-dollar development project including investment in rail and port infrastructure stretching from China to Europe. Also known as the One Belt and One Road initiative.

nominated deal in the international energy market. At the 2014 APEC summit meeting held in Beijing, China's president Xi Jinping proposed several measures to accelerate the long-sought initiative of creating a Free Trade Area of the Asia-Pacific.

China has also supported a new Asian security concept. President Xi characterized the concept at the 2014 CICA[4] summit meeting held in Shanghai: it calls for the people of Asia to run the affairs of Asia, solve the problems of Asia, and uphold the security of Asia.

The U.S. is not in a position to block the series of initiatives introduced by China. Instead, it has been deepening its engagement with China to try to manage and coordinate the interests of both sides.

Japan-China Relations
The economic power balance between Japan and China has shifted significantly while the diplomatic relations of the two have deteriorated over several issues, including the dispute over the Senkaku/Diaoyu Islands, the official prime ministerial visits to the controversial Yasukuni Shrine, and the interpretation of wartime history.

Japan's GDP was surpassed by China's in 2010. According to the IMF, the GDP gap between the two was estimated to double in 2014 and to triple by 2019. The troubled economic relations have caused huge damage to both sides. We cannot afford to continue on this path of confrontation.

The Japanese government, upon U.S. urging, has decided to stay out of the AIIB. The decision shows Japan's serious problem: maintaining a narrow perspective on global issues tied to U.S. influence. Japan, in its refusal to join, raises questions about the AIIB regarding trans-

---

4 Conference on Interaction and Confidence-Building Measures in Asia. CICA is a multilateral forum for enhancing cooperation in Asia. 26 states join the forum while 7 nations including Japan as well as 4 international organizations take part in it as observers. It was founded in 1993 and its secretariat office is in Almaty, Kazakhstan.

parency on the management of the bank or its funding standards. Those issues, however, can be solved through negotiation. The actual reason for Japan's decision was its reluctance to accept China as a major power or to help China become one.

The U.S. and its Western allies recognize the potential consequences of Chinese economic expansion and respond in pursuit of their own national interests.

Japan, however, appears to be in denial regarding China's rise, sticking to an outdated stance of confrontation and refuses to acknowledge the reality. To put it another way, Japan is still trapped in an outdated elitist attitude that proclaims Japan is No. 1 in Asia, and is unable to psychologically bridge the gap between Japan in today's world and what Japan used to be in the past. As a result, the sentiment of the Japanese political elite is to continue its rivalry with China, and their policy line is to counter China in any way possible. While Japan's business circle seeks to deal with the situation realistically to benefit its own interests, Japan's outdated politics gets in the way.

Tokyo's counter-China strategy is unlikely to be considered productive in the broader international arena. Even the U.S. is reluctant to align its policies with Japan's confrontational stance against China although it demands that Japan play a larger military role worldwide. The U.S. government points out that to escalate tensions between Japan and China is a serious mistake, calling for both sides to take measures toward a diplomatic resolution of disputes. This U.S. stance is not compatible with the Abe administration's which puts an enhanced Japan-U.S. alliance at the core of its counter-China strategy.

If Japan intensifies its policy into an overall anti-China strategy, no other nation will support it and this could alienate Japan from the international community of nations.

Wartime History Rewritten

The Abe administration has another yet more serious issue to overcome and that is Mr. Abe's interpretation of Japan's wartime history which had led to increasing friction with other governments and international civil societies.

This issue has created uneasiness even in some Asian governments that usually refrain from publicly commenting on issues such as Mr. Abe's controversial push to revise the Constitution. This indicates that they have serious concerns over the nationalistic and ultra-conservative nature of the administration reminiscent of the wartime past.

If the Abe government refuses to acknowledge and repudiate the fascism and militarism associated with WWII; if it refuses to accept the history that Japan committed a war of aggression and colonial rule over Asia; if it refuses to stop the glorification of Japan's wartime conduct in line with Mr. Abe's personal beliefs, then, Japan will be seen as a threat to the current international order. It is absolutely necessary for Japan to overcome this issue if it wants to regain international trust.

As this year marks the 70th anniversary since the end of the WWII, the Japanese Communist Party has identified five points regarding the basic stance the Japanese government should take in order to promote harmony and friendship with other Asian countries.

The JCP calls on the government to:

①abide by the core content of the Murayama Statement and the Kono Statement, act in accordance with the principles shown in the statements, and refute arguments by opponents of the statements;

②implement measures to restore the dignity of victims of Japan's wartime sex slave system, including offering official apologies and compensation;

③make a rule banning lawmakers—in particular, cabinet members—from making official Yasukuni Shrine visits which are tantamount to justifying the past war of aggression;

④take a firm stance and legislate against racist hate speech demonstrations; and

⑤authorize the publication and use of history textbooks that accurately reflect the government's stance on the aggressive war as presented in the Murayama and Kono statements.

C, Cooperation among Japan, South Korea and China

There are three main challenges to be addressed in Northeast Asia: to soundly build mutual trust and respect; to carefully and diplomatically deal with territorial disputes; and to work with neighbors to adjust regional relations. In order to address the changing relations in the region, we need to establish a multilateral security framework to preserve peace and stability to meet the challenges associated with changes in the regional relations.

1, Japan

Japan's counter-China orientation engenders a tendency to seek more military-leaning measures instead of measures supporting the peaceful resolution of conflicts. Japan's current foreign policy is far removed from Japan's postwar constitution with its pacifist ideal and certainly does not resonate with the ASEAN emphasis on peaceful diplomacy. Rather, it goes in the opposite direction by insisting on exercising the right to collective self-defense that will enable Japan to once again engage in wars abroad.

This creates a bulwark against the establishment of peace and stability in East Asia and is further exacerbated by the present government campaign to justify Japan's past aggressive war. Japanese public opinion clearly opposes this move[5].

2, China

The Japanese Communist Party has enumerated the following points in order to help improve Japan's relations with China.

Firstly, Japan and China should recognize the existence of the territorial disputes and make efforts to find solutions through cool-headed diplomatic negotiations.

Secondly, Japan and China should refrain from initiating military responses to the disputes which change the current conditions.

Thirdly, Japan and China should make efforts to prevent territorial disputes from affecting bilateral economic relations as well as personal and cultural exchanges.

We strongly hope that China will continue to develop peacefully, be trusted by neighboring countries, avoid objectionable rhetoric, and meet the expectations of a major power.[6]

---

5   According to a recent poll conducted by the Nikkei in May 2015, only 31% of respondents are in favor of a bill to allow the exercise of the right to collective self-defense and 51% oppose. Another survey by NHK shows 23% in favor, 35% against.
6   I had an opportunity to make a speech titled "Politics in Japan and Environment for Peace in Northeast Asia" at the 4th World Socialism Forum held in Beijing in October 2013. I pointed out, "As China is developing into a strong power, China is also raising expectations for assuming more responsibility in world affairs. In this regard, I believe that winning respect and trust from neighboring countries as well as the international community will be one of China's high priorities. In other words, the world is anticipating China taking a responsible role with the power of virtue. To put it in the Chinese manner, the power of virtue I mentioned here means to embrace wangdao, the virtuous and moral way, and to reject badao, the coercive way. Winning the trust of the world, I believe, belongs to wangdao. There is a proverb in Japan: the more rice grows, the lower its ears hang. As China is becoming a global power, the world is looking forward to seeing China use its strengthened power and increased influence judiciously with restraint and virtue."

3, For Peace and Cooperation in Northeast Asia

The Japanese Communist Party proposes a new initiative for peace and cooperation in Northeast Asia as follows:

- Conclude a Treaty of Amity and Cooperation in Northeast Asia with rules for peace which member countries need to abide by, including renunciation of the use of force, peaceful resolution of conflicts, non-interference in the internal affairs of other countries, and promotion of meaningful dialogues and cooperation for confidence building.

- Return to the Joint Statement of the Six-Party Talks issued in September 2005, create a nuclear-free Korean Peninsula, realize a comprehensive resolution on nuclear weapons, missiles, and the abduction issue as well as unsolved historical issues, and develop this framework into one that can create and maintain peace and stability in Northeast Asia.

- Engage in diplomatic negotiations in a calm manner based on historical facts and international law as the means to solve territorial disputes existing in the region. Strictly refrain from actions that could escalate into conflicts, such as any forcible change in the status quo and use or threat to use force, and conclude a code of conduct for the countries concerned to solve conflicts through friendly consultations and negotiations in accordance with international law.

- Japan's remorse over its past war of aggression and colonial rule is the essential basis to develop amity and cooperation in Northeast Asia. Swiftly resolve Japan's military sexual slavery issue and other unresolved issues and block the rise of adverse forces trying to falsify the historical record[7].

We have received positive responses to our proposal in exchanges with officials in foreign governments as well as foreign political parties.

7　Adopted in the 26th JCP congress in January 2014. See http://www.jcp.or.jp/english/jps_2014/20140118_26th_congress.html

Last October, Japanese Communist Party Chair Kazuo Shii presented this proposal in a speech at Korea University in Seoul. There is much more to do in order to spread and gain support for the concept of establishing a peaceful East Asian Community.

We regard our proposal as a practical approach to enable the establishment of such a community.

Firstly, President Park Geun-hye of South Korea also proposed an initiative similar to ours regarding peace and cooperation in Northeast Asia[8] . Her proposal gained support from several governments including China.

Secondly, while the Japanese Communist Party believes that Japan should break away from its military alliance with the U.S., our proposal is achievable even if the Japan-U.S. alliance or the U.S.-ROK alliance remains in place. Our proposal can gain support from across the political spectrum regardless of the stance taken on the military alliances.

Thirdly, we have the example of another once conflict-stricken region, Latin America, which has succeeded in establishing the regional community of CELAC, similar in many ways to ASEAN's peace initiative, built on the historical aspiration for enabling a peaceful resolution of conflicts without intervention from outside powers. I think this shows that the trend for establishing regional integration into communities of peace has become a global reality.

I hope we work together to enrich the ideals and spirit behind the move to establish a peaceful East Asian Community through fruitful discussions and forward momentum enhanced by a deeper understanding

---

8   President Park presented her initiative at the joint session of U.S. Congress in 2013. She proposed to build a mechanism of peace and cooperation in Northeast Asia through a series of extended multilateral dialogue and confidence-building measures starting with softer issues including environment, disaster relief and counter-terrorism.

of the world situation.

5, Cooperation for Peace in Northeast Asia

International Conference on Peace and Space for Global Security and Human Development
Gandhi Institute of Technical and Management Studies (GITAM University),
November 18-20, 2016, Visakhapatnam, India

Distinguished guests,
Dear comrades and friends,

It is the great honor for me to be invited to the International Conference on Peace & Space for Global Security and Human Development at Gandhi Institute of Technical and Management Studies (GITAM University) in Visakhapatnam.

First of all, I would like to express my gratitude to kind invitation and warm hospitality for us.

I would like to make a modest contribution by focusing on two subjects; one is on the present situation surrounding the nuclear weapons issue and our task to realize a world without nuclear weapons. The other is on our task to improve the instable situation in Northeast Asia and finally to make the region a peaceful area as part of Asian Union for peaceful and economic advantages.

Firstly, as co-chairperson of the World Conference against A & H Bombs, which holds annual conferences at Hiroshima and Nagasaki every August, I heartily welcome a recent epoch-making development which could open the door to a world without nuclear weapons.

On August 19, the United Nations Open-Ended Working Group (OEWG) on Disarmament adopted a report that calls on the U.N. General Assembly to take concrete measures in 2017 to start international negotiations for the creation of a convention to ban and eliminate nuclear weapons.

In response to that, on October 28, the United Nations First Committee adopted the resolution that also recommends the U.N. General Assembly to convene "a conference in 2017, open to all States, with the participation and contribution of international organizations and civil society, to negotiate a legally binding instrument to prohibit nuclear weapons, leading towards their total elimination." In coming December, the General Assembly will likely adopt a resolution following the First Committee recommendations.

This is to aim to substantively discuss concrete and effective legal measures, legal provisions and norms that needs to be included in a treaty to attain and maintain a world without nuclear weapons.

Indeed, to ban and eliminate nuclear weapons by a treaty is the long-standing core demand of the international anti-atom movements. Now is the time to make every possible effort to build overwhelming public support to achieve this goal.

The coming conference in the United Nations will be open to the civil society organizations. We will participate in it together with the Hibakusha who have suffered from the Atomic-bombing.

To raise the anti-atom public opinion, we have attached much importance to the inhumane consequences caused by using atomic bombs. The seventy-one years ago, the United States used nuclear weapons for the first time against humanity in Hiroshima and Nagasaki. With tremendous destructive power and radiation, the bombs burned out the two cities and claimed nearly 210,000 lives by the end of the year. It was a hell on earth. The Hibakusha who survived then had to suffer from latent effects of radiation and social discrimination for many subsequent years. Such inhumane weapons must not be used in any circumstances whatsoever. I have a strong conviction that nuclear weapons cannot and should not ever coexist with humanity.

The nuclear-weapon states still maintain more than 15,000 nuclear warheads. A recent study shows that even if only a small percentage of existing nuclear weapons are used, it would cause, among other devastating effects, serious climate change which would bring the human race to the brink of extinction. The elimination of nuclear weapons is the urgent task for the very survival of the humanity.

We have been conducting an international campaign that calls for immediate ban on nuclear weapons by international law and justice, more specifically, by concluding an international convention to prohibit nuclear weapons.

Now, weapons of mass destruction are widely perceived to be illegal, as biological and chemical weapons have been banned by international treaties. Why not nuclear weapons!

The international conferences on the inhumane nature of nuclear weapons were held three times in Mexico, Norway and Austria with attendance of representatives from various governments as well as NGOs. And in the 2015 NPT Review Conference at the United Nations, the majority opinion was that the international community must take legal steps as "effective measures" required by Article VI of the NPT based on deep recognition of the inhumane nature of nuclear weapons. Although the 2015 Review Conference failed to adopt its final documents, the draft of them reflected the majority opinion to a large degree.

These new developments are along the line of progress that worldwide anti-nuclear-weapon movements have long been calling on the world to make. What underlies in the international cooperation and efforts in this regard is the deep awareness of "the inhumane nature of nuclear weapons" which the tragedies of Hiroshima and Nagasaki revealed.

The political battle map over the issue of elimination of nuclear weapons is clear. 70% of all NPT member states stand for efforts to create a legal framework aiming for the ban and elimination of nuclear weapons. On the other hand, the Permanent Five (P-5) states which have an exclusive "right" to possess nuclear weapons, namely the U.S., Russia, China, France, the U.K, are working together to block and suppress the global effort towards elimination of nuclear weapons.

The P-5 states opposed the establishment of the OEWG at the U.N. They argue, "A step-by-step approach is the only practical option for making progress towards nuclear disarmament". They also insist, "Addressing further prospects for nuclear disarmament would require taking into account all factors that could affect global strategic stability." This kind of argument means that they just want to postpone the total elimination of nuclear weapons to an indefinite future. In practice, they are against the total abolishment of nuclear weapons.

The P-5 states, which have become very active and unified as a group at NPT-related meetings since 2009, intimidates other governments and anti-nuclear movements by saying, "A ban without the support and participation of the nuclear-weapon states would not eliminate nuclear weapons, but would rather undermine the NPT regime."

The Japanese government abstained from voting on the establishment of the OEWG, and opposed the resolution of the UN first Committee that recommends the U.N. General Assembly to convene a conference in 2017 to discuss a nuclear weapons convention.

In essence, the Japanese government just spoke on behalf of the P-5 states and insisted "to attain real progress in nuclear disarmament, it is essential to ensure the united actions of the entire community, including the nuclear-weapon states." It also stated, "We need a focus on not just humanitarian but also security considerations."

It is the movements and public opinion of the peoples of the world that are the driving force to open a nuclear-weapon-free, peaceful and just future.

The World Conference against A&H Bombs held last August in Hiroshima and Nagasaki announced the launch of the "International Signature Campaign in Support of the Appeal of the Hibakusha, the Atomic Bomb Survivors of Hiroshima & Nagasaki, for the Elimination of Nuclear Weapons." Its aim is to forge strong public opinion demanding a treaty to ban and eliminate nuclear weapons and its goal is to collect hundreds of millions of signatures worldwide. To help promote these actions, we will continue to make widely known the damage of Hiroshima and Nagasaki and help Hibakusha to share their experiences with people around the world.

We need to strengthen our solidarity with all movements on various fronts including opposition to war and promotion of peace, reduction and dismantling of foreign military bases from Okinawa, Guam, Diego Garcia and other places, effective control of arms trade and military industry, cuts in military expenditures, improvement of living conditions, employment and social welfare, overcoming poverty and disparity, prevention of climate change, protection of global environment, elimination of sexism and other discriminations, overcoming social injustice and realizing sustainable development.

Ladies and gentlemen,

Next, I would like to discuss how we can create cooperation for peace in Northeast Asia.

The region faces potential conflicts and increased tensions. It has a series of destabilizing factors including nuclear and ballistic missile programs of North Korea, deteriorating Japan-China relations, straining Japan-Korea relations, strengthened U.S. military deployment in Japan, and historical issues on war of aggression by Japan.

In this regard, the Japanese Communist Party has proposed an initiative for peace and cooperation in Northeast Asia. We have made the following proposals in the 26th party congress held in January 2014.

①- Conclude a Treaty of Amity and Cooperation in Northeast Asia as rules for peace, to promote peaceful solution of conflicts, and effective dialogues and cooperation for confidence building.

②- Realize a comprehensive resolution on North Korean issues under the framework of Six Party Talk, and develop this framework into one that attains and maintains peace and stability in Northeast Asia.

③- Stick to diplomatic negotiations to solve territorial disputes existing in the region, and conclude a code of conduct for the countries concerned.

④- Japan should express remorse over its past war of aggression and colonial rule as the essential basis to develop amity and cooperation in Northeast Asia.

These are the main points in our proposal. It is intended to increase efforts to create an ASEAN-type regional cooperation of nations for peace in Northeast Asia. I believe our initiative offers a practical way to bring about peace and stability in the region.

We are exchanging views on our proposal with other governmental or party officials in various nations and have received positive responses. I will continue to make efforts to realize this initiative and would like all of you here in this hall to kindly pay attention to our proposal.

In order to create a peace order in Northeast Asia, I would like to emphasize two important points.

First, we must avoid being caught in a vicious cycle in which military measures invite further military countermeasures. If there is a provocative military act which violates the U.N. Charter and the international law, such an act should be strongly condemned. And the best way to reach a resolution is by means of diplomacy through dialogue. We must persevere in seeking a diplomatic and peaceful solution to any conflict. When we are not wise enough to have other options than reacting militarily or enhancing military deterrence, we will only invite a military reaction. We must refrain from putting our nations at risk of being trapped in a dangerous path toward military escalation.

Second, on territorial disputes, we must refrain from conducting any act which could escalate tensions, including threat or use of force and unilateral change of status quo by coercive measures. It is imperative for us to seek solutions patiently through negotiations and consultations in a peaceful manner. This is what the U.N. Charter and the universally recognized principles of international law require us to do.

In this sense, China is strongly requested to act to seek a peaceful solution of the conflicts in accordance with the international law.

We believe that Japan should take an important role to contribute to crafting a peaceful region in Northeast Asia, which is now unfortunately supposed to be one of potential instable areas that could trigger military conflict.

We are determined to make utmost effort to advance for peace in Asia and beyond with this initiative. Thank you for your attention.

6, Politics in Japan and Environment for Peace in Northeast Asia

4th World Socialism Forum by Chinese Academy of Social Sciences
October 30-31, 2013, Beijing, China

A, What the Upper House Election Revealed

In the Upper House election of Japan held July 21, the Liberal Democratic Party (LDP) gained 65 seats out of 121. The LDP earned 18.46 million votes in the proportional representation system. Combined with their seats that were not part of the election this year, the LDP and its junior coalition partner the New Komeito now have a stable majority in the Upper House. After Prime Minister Shinzo Abe assumed office in December last year, the Diet was divided between the LDP-New Komeito-controlled Lower House and the opposition-controlled Upper House. As a result of the election, the ruling coalition parties have now regained a majority in both Houses.

The Democratic Party of Japan (DPJ) sharply lost support from voters. Three years ago, it gained 18.45 million votes. But this year, it got only 7.13 million votes, winning only 17 seats. In the last decade, the DPJ was expected to become a major party in a new "two-party system" in Japan. The ruling establishment eagerly wanted to see a "two-party system" in which two similar parties like the LDP and the DPJ take turns running the government. Nevertheless, after the DPJ administration of 3 years, Japanese voters lost confidence in the DPJ and even hated it for its incompetence of governing and then breaking its election pledges to the voters. Through the reviewing process of the election results, the DPJ itself confided in a party document that the DPJ has become "a party rejected by people". The DPJ has a critical weakness in that it lacks the ability to differentiate itself from the LDP in policy matters.

The Japan Restoration Party gained 6.25 million votes and won 8

Chapter1 The Way to Peace and Security in East Asia

seats. However, this party failed to keep the momentum that had lifted it up to the third largest party in the Lower House last year. The party lost its appeal as a "third force" competing with the LDP and the DPJ. Even a co-founder of the party said the Japan Restoration Party had passed its "expiration date". Your Party, which is seen as another "third force" party, had 4.75 million votes and won 8 seats. This party also failed to keep the momentum that had seen them double their seats in the Lower House last year. Both parties have been talking much about changing the "existing party system". Yet the reality is that they themselves are parties within the "existing party system" and just supplementary forces to the LDP. Both parties take almost the same position as the LDP's on a lot of issues such as historical understanding, the proposed revision of the Japanese Constitution or the Trans-Pacific Partnership negotiations.

The Japanese Communist Party (JCP) won 8 seats in total. The JCP gained 5.15 million votes in the proportional representation system, which is 9.7% of the total votes cast, securing 5 seats. The JCP got the second largest number of votes following the LDP in Tokyo Metropolis and Kyoto prefecture. The JCP candidates also won in 3 major local constituencies, Japan's capital Tokyo, an important commercial city, Osaka, and a famous historic city Kyoto. Just before the Upper House election, the JCP had already made another advance in the Tokyo Metropolitan Assembly election. The party increased its seats from 8 to 17. Now, the youngest member of the Upper House and the youngest member of the Tokyo Metropolitan Assembly are both female politicians of the Japanese Communist Party. The former is 30 years old and the latter is 25 years old. Much of the major news media in Japan have paid close attention to the JCP's success.

The gap between the LDP-gained votes and the JCP-gained votes has now narrowed to around 3.5 to 1 in the proportional representation system. Politics in Japan is now often said to enter an era of confrontation between the Japanese Communist Party and the Liberal Democratic Party. Political analysts have commonly pointed out that Japanese voters can now clearly see that only the JCP can be counted on as a firm opposition party to square off directly with the LDP while the so-called "new two-party system" or the "third force" parties have lost their appeal to the voters. A lot of voters commented that they had no alternative but to vote for the JCP in order to express their resentment against the LDP-led politics. One of the characteristics of the election was that the role and policy of the Japanese Communist Party became clearer in the voters' eyes.

B, Post-Election Politics in Japan---Contradiction between the Administration and the People

As I said earlier, after assuming office in December last year, the LDP and its junior coalition partner the New Komeito now have a stable majority in both the Upper and Lower Houses. That means that theoretically, they have the power to pass any bill regardless of public support or opposition. The Abe administration, infected with a traditional political disease in Japan, subordination to the United States, has a long policy list. This includes strengthening Japan-U.S. military cooperation, joining the Trans-Pacific Partnership (TPP) negotiations at the expense of the sovereignty of Japan, nurturing a reactionary trend to justify and glorify the past war of aggression caused by a militarist Japan, revising the Japanese Constitution to remove its pacifism, creating a National Defense Force and exercising the right to collective self-defense.

But this policy agenda does not have public support. So, it is unlikely that the administration can do whatever it wants easily. When you look at the level of the public support for the LDP more carefully, the LDP gained only 18% support among all eligible voters in the proportional representation system. According to an opinion poll conducted by the Nikkei newspaper, only 17% was the public support for the proposed consumption tax hike from 5% to 8% in 2014 and 10% in 2015. The support for the exercise of the right to collective self-defense was only 32%. This trend is common among various opinion polls and the level of support for such policies is in gradual decline. There has been strong opposition among voters against participation in the TPP and a majority of people has opposed revision of Article 9 of the Japanese Constitution. In this way, you can see the seriously widening gap in policy matters between the LDP and the Japanese people, even though the LDP was believed to have won a landslide election victory.

During the election campaign, the LDP practically kept its mouth shut about its political agenda and put forward an economic policy called "Abenomics". The LDP loudly claimed that the party successfully turned the Japanese economy in the right direction resulting in high stock prices and a weak yen. Although "Abenomics" itself is widely criticized for its inevitable failure in the near future, the LDP gambled with the policy to win the votes before its failure would become clear.

It is unavoidable that contradiction between the Abe administration and the Japanese people will be sharpening. We must stop the LDP policy agenda by influencing public opinion and supporting a movement against it and I think it is possible. We can see in this point both danger and an opportunity for a new political course for Japan. Such opportunity must be seized by people's will and efforts.

C, Contradiction between the Abe Administration and the World

1, The Issue of Historical Understanding

The Abe administration has another serious contradiction. Prime Minister Abe's historical perspective and his view of the world order stand in contradiction with international public opinion and that of not a small number of governments in the world.

Concerns about Abe's view have now been expressed by even some Asian countries that usually keep a low-key approach to issues such as revision of the Japanese Constitution. But they are now publicly alarmed by the nationalistic and extremely right-leaning trend that the Abe administration has been pursuing. Those countries have shown explicitly their deep concerns over Japan's political tilting to the right.

This situation in Japan has set off alarm bells in international opinion, too. The New York Times warned in an editorial on July 22, the day just after the Upper House election, "Mr. Abe should not treat the [election] results as an endorsement of his disturbingly right-wing foreign-policy views, which include a nationalistic revision of World War II history, overheated rhetoric toward China and attempts to rewrite Japan's Constitution to permit more assertive military actions. This election was about economics." Such arguments are becoming common among major world news media.

If the Abe administration does not endorse the international repudiation of fascism and militarism as a foundation of the Post-World-War-II international order, and if the Abe administration wrong-headedly continues to justify the past military aggression towards and colonization of Asia, it will commit a serious mistake in anachronistically becoming a reactionary force against the current international order.

Prime Minister Abe told the Diet, "The definition of the war of aggression has not yet been determined either internationally or academically. Countries have different views on it." In addition to that, four cabinet members, including Vice Prime Minister Taro Aso, visited the Yasukuni Shrine this spring. Mr. Aso also made a controversial comment that if we examine the Nazis' political maneuvers, we can obtain clues on how to revise the Japanese Constitution. These facts have clearly shown that the historical perspective of the Abe cabinet is completely different from that commonly held in the international community. The historical views of the Abe cabinet are based on ignorance of principles of the United Nations Charter and the very raison d'être of the U.N. Mr. Abe's view also undermines the common basis on which the Post-World-War-II-Order has been built. This situation has raised doubts about the political and diplomatic credibility of Japan.

2, Destabilizing Factors in Northeast Asia and Japan-U.S. Relationship

Enhancing peace and stability in Northeast Asia is now an increasingly important challenge for us. There are destabilizing factors in the region such as the nuclear issue of North Korea, which has already declared itself a nuclear power, the territorial dispute in the East China Sea between Japan and China, the enhanced U.S. military bases and deployment under the ongoing realignment of U.S. forces and so on. But today, I would like to talk about how Japan's diplomacy has been distorted by the historical perspective issue.

High-level communication between Japan and China or between Japan and South Korea has been brought to a halt. This situation is a serious loss for all parties. Economic cooperation as well as people's exchanges has been prevented, too. In addition to that, even trilateral meetings among the U.S., China and South Korea, but not including Japan, have taken place.

The United States has embraced a basic strategy called "the strategic rebalance toward Asia." Under the strategy, the U.S. approach toward China is to integrate China deeply into the current international order while, as a hedge, keeping the U.S. military posture in the region, along with strengthened alliances with countries such as Japan. The U.S. sees the concerns caused by Abe's historical perspective and subsequent friction with the neighboring countries as obstacles for implementation of its own Asia strategy. The U.S. has real concerns that such issues could have an adverse impact on the entire security environment in Northeast Asia.

In a sense, it might be safe to say that the U.S. administration is now facing a challenge on how to deal effectively with the political crisis in Northeast Asia that Mr. Abe has caused by his historical revisionism.

The issue of the so-called "comfort women," who are the victims of the sex slavery system for Japan Imperial Army soldiers in Asia during the war time, was a serious violation of universal human rights. But Prime Minister Abe has denied the responsibility of the Japanese government for that conduct. This denial has come from his strong-held

55

"values" in which he has no regret or no remorse for the past military aggression and the colonization over Asia by the imperial Japan. These peculiar values of his have brought a lot of criticism from all over the world. The irony is that Mr. Abe has promoted his diplomatic engagement with Northeast Asia as "Value-Based Diplomacy." Clearly, he is walking a path leading to alienation from the rest of the world, which could undermine Japan's diplomatic clout.

Such counter-China diplomacy of the Abe administration has cast a shadow over Japan-U.S. relations. Mr. Abe visited the U.S. in February to meet with President Obama. The U.S. used Japan as an ally while the U.S. carefully avoided giving any support to Mr. Abe's ideology. The U.S. reportedly prepared for the meeting with Mr. Abe, deliberately not sharing anti-China views with him, as well as not expressing a need for exercising the right to collective self-defense, both of which Japan wanted to put on the agenda.

As has been reported widely, the U.S. government recently expressed its welcome for Japan's consideration for exercising the right to collective self-defense in the Joint Statement of the Security Consultative Committee issued on October 3 after the foreign and defense ministerial meeting in Tokyo. But if you see it in the right context, you can understand a nuanced approach of the U.S. Clearly, the U.S. puts importance to the Japan-U.S. alliance as a basis of its forward-deployed strategy in Asia Pacific region. While the U.S. wants to have meaningful deterrence and influence over China, it does not want to jeopardize U.S.-China relationship by going with Japan's intention to constrain China by focusing on strengthening the Japan-U.S. military alliance. U.S. Secretary of State John Kerry told at the joint press conference in Tokyo, "We seek to have a relationship with China that's based on an understanding of the ways in which we can find cooperation on the major issues." This showed a difference between Japanese government's intention and the U.S. current strategic focus.

Mr. Abe has been criticized for not visiting the Yasukuni Shrine from his political bases. But if he visits the shrine, then there is no doubt that he will face criticism from the U.S., the ally. Clearly, he is in a serious dilemma.

Even though he has a stable majority in the Diet, his political position is unstable. This is a paradox. The Abe administration now faces serious contradictions with the Japanese people as well as the world.

D, For Peace and Stability in Northeast Asia

This is not the first time when issues related to historical understanding triggered international concerns and diplomatic problems. Former Prime Minister Jun-ichiro Koizumi repeatedly visited the Yasukuni Shrine during his tenure and caused such problems. The JCP criticized his conduct and actively demanded that he not visit the shrine. This time too, the JCP has actively squared off against such historical revisionism as promoted by Mr. Abe.

The Japanese government should sincerely regret the past unjust war of aggression. This is the foundation on which we can build a peaceful and stable Northeast Asia. Japan can form a deep and lasting friendship with countries in the Northeast Asia only by squarely facing its own past and learning lessons from it for a better future.

1, Resolving Disputes through Diplomacy
Having said that, what is urgently needed for peace and stability in Northeast Asia is to enhance efforts to resolve all disputes and tensions through skilled and mature politics and diplomacy.

The region should carefully avoid being caught in a vicious circle of military escalation and should take a course toward disarmament instead of maintaining an arms race. In order to do so, the region should also leave behind the old security concept of military balance or force-to-force approach.

Every country in the East Asia has developed its own bilateral relations. China and the United States have been deepening economic ties as well as people's exchanges through institutionalizing the Strategic and Economic Dialogue. Everybody knows now that there will and can be no war between China and the U.S.

Unfortunately, however, the relationship between Japan and China is complicated. It is urgently needed for both countries to return to "the mutually beneficial relationship based on common strategic interests", which Mr. Abe himself agreed on with Chinese leaders in 2006. When there is a territorial dispute between both countries, what is critically important for addressing such an issue is to pursue a diplomatic solution with perseverance based on historical facts and international law. If both countries continue to handle such an issue in a coercive manner with force, it could lead to an escalation and unintentional, serious consequences. Regrettably, that would only amplify mutual distrust and increase the tension.

The JCP believes that Japan's possession of the Senkaku Islands (Diaoyu Islands in Chinese) is legitimate based on history and international law. At the same time, given the fact that there remains the territorial dispute between Japan and China, the only and best way to solve the dispute is to have cool-headed, rational dialogue between the two countries.

The JCP has demanded that the Japanese and Chinese governments make rational decisions based on a broad perspective in order to maintain a healthy and friendly bilateral relationship and the JCP has proposed the following 3 principles:

Firstly, Japan and China should recognize the existence of the territorial dispute and make efforts to find a solution through cool-headed diplomatic negotiations.

Secondly, Japan and China should strictly refrain from initiating physical and military responses which would change the current conditions.

Thirdly, Japan and China should make efforts to prevent this issue from affecting bilateral economic relations as well as personal and cultural exchanges.

The JCP is convinced that a solution through diplomatic negotiations in accord with these three principles as one package is the only way to resolve the issue.

2, ASEAN's Experience and Peace in Northeast Asia

I think the experience that the Association of Southeast Asian Nations (ASEAN) has gained is important and helpful for building and maintaining peace in the Northeast Asia. ASEAN has now developed into a regional community that takes various initiatives for peace and economic development in such a politically, historically and religiously diverse region. They have already left behind the era full of wars and hostilities with one another.

They have created a multilateral security framework for the region through a multi-layered architecture based on the Treaty of Amity and Cooperation in Southeast Asia (TAC) like the ASEAN Regional Forum (ARF), the East Asia Summit (EAS) and others. The core principle for them is diplomacy in promoting bilateral and multilateral dialogues and consensus-building to solve whatever problems or differences they have.

We believe that it is important to expand such efforts ASEAN has made to Northeast Asia. As you all know, Northeast Asia does not have any established institution like ASEAN at the moment. But the region has a framework called "the Six-Party Talks" that was originally launched for denuclearization of North Korea. Although the talks have been halted for 5 years, the Six-Party Talks is still the only framework that has the potential to become a multilateral architecture in the Northeast Asia for solving problems in the region beyond North Korea.

In September 2005, a Joint Statement was issued with the Six-Party Talks reiterating the goal of making the Korean Peninsula nuclear-free while aiming to become a multilateral framework to create peace and stability in the Northeast Asia. If the region goes back to this Joint Statement and makes good on its own commitment, it will be possible to develop this framework into a regional community for peace in Northeast Asia. Such a development would be an outlook that everyone really appreciates for the future of the region.

3, China's Growing Role

China's role has been growing in Northeast Asia and everywhere else in the world. The Chinese economy has grown visibly and rapidly. It already surpassed the Japanese economy in 2010 in terms of gross domestic product (GDP). China is now the second largest economy in the world. You cannot understand global phenomena such as rise of the South or structural changes in the world economy unless you take into account China's role.

While the United States wants to keep its current status as the global superpower, China is expected to surpass even the U.S. economy in the long term. Some observers even have pointed out a possibility that the world will experience for the first time in history a peaceful transition of the ranking order among the big global powers. If so, it will become all the more important for China to take a path of "peaceful development" as has been committed to by China itself.

As China is developing into a strong power, China is also raising expectations for assuming more responsibility in world affairs. In this regard, I believe that winning respect and trust from neighboring countries as well as the international community would be one of China's high priorities. In other words, the world is anticipating China taking a responsible role with the power of virtue.

To put it in the Chinese manner, the power of virtue I mentioned here means to embrace "wangdao" (in Chinese), the virtuous and moral way, and to reject "badao", the coercive way. Winning the trust of the world, I believe, belongs to "wangdao". There is a proverb in Japan, saying "the more rice grows, the lower its ears hang." As China is becoming a global power, the world is looking forward to seeing China use its strengthened power and increased influence judiciously, with restraint and virtue.

Northeast Asia has a huge potential. If every country in the region makes common and shared efforts to solve all disputes through dialogue, the region will make a great advance toward being a prosperous community optimizing its economic potential with peace, mutual respect for sovereignty and mutual benefits. There is no doubt about it. We, the Japanese Communist Party, are determined to make utmost efforts to create such a community for peace in this region and for Japan to play an important role in it.

Chapter II

World Peace and Elimination of Nuclear Weapons

1, Historical adoption of the Treaty on the Prohibition of Nuclear Weapons

2017 World Conference against A and H Bombs
August 3, 2017, Hiroshima

This year's world conference is taking place under the new situation in which the Treaty on the Prohibition of Nuclear Weapons was adopted at the U.N. conference in July. Over many years, the world conference has worked together with Hibakusha (A-bomb survivors) to raise awareness of the inhumanity of atomic bombs and has promoted signature campaigns calling for a "treaty to ban and eliminate nuclear weapons", including the International Signature Campaign in Support of the Appeal of the Hibakusha. We are very glad to have made an important contribution with Hibakusha toward realizing this historic achievement.

What is important now is planning our future activities based on this achievement - how to make progress from the ban to total abolition of nuclear weapons. I want to stress the following three points:

First is to increase awareness of the epoch-making and progressive importance of the nuclear weapons ban treaty and strengthen world opinion in support of this pact.

The preamble of the convention condemns the inhumane nature of nuclear arms, making clear the unlawfulness of the weapons in light of established legal principles of the global community, including international humanitarian law.

Article 1 of the treaty bans each state party from developing, testing, producing, manufacturing, acquiring, possessing, or stockpiling nuclear weapons, and also disallows the stationing, installation or deployment of the arms in its territory or at any place under its jurisdiction or control. It also prohibits the use or threat to use the weapons. This provision is highly significant as it nullifies the nuclear deterrence argument. Thus, nuclear weapons have been outlawed for the first time in history, branded as evil.

The accord refers to "Hibakusha" twice and stipulates "assistance for the victims of the use or testing of nuclear weapons", in response to our long-held demand to provide assistance to A-bomb survivors.

The delegation of the Japanese Communist Party joined in the discussions held at the U.N. conference as a member of Parliamentarians for Nuclear Non-Proliferation and Disarmament (PNND). We could see bright prospects for the future of the world by closely observing Hibakusha and civil society's intellectual and practical contribution to the debate as well as the process of governments coming together to deepen mutual trust and respect. This treaty has become an advanced one which reflects the process in which national governments and civil society made united efforts to create it based on the principles of democracy in international politics. It also stresses the importance of gender equality for the future.

Second is to develop the campaign to progress from the ban to total elimination of nuclear weapons as the signature and ratification procedures will start soon.

Article 12 of the pact states that "Each State Party shall encourage States not party to this Treaty to sign, ratify, accept, approve or accede to the Treaty." This provision expands the area in which state parties and civil society can collaborate to advance new international efforts.

The governments of Lebanon and Cyprus, which I visited last month, both voted for the treaty. When I met with a senior official of Cyprus' Foreign Ministry, we shared our joy at the treaty adoption and agreed to enhance our mutual cooperation. I also met with representatives of pacifist organizations in the two countries and we agreed to work together to increase signatories to the convention.

Third is, with the norms of the treaty, to put increasing pressure on nuclear states and their allies to become a party to the treaty, which opens the door to all U.N. members.

Three allied nuclear powers – the U.S., Britain, and France – issued a joint statement criticizing the adopted pact. The statement rationalizes their possession of nuclear arms on the pretext of North Korea's nuclear development program, claiming yet again that the shared goal of nuclear disarmament should be attained by a "step-by-step approach" while promoting strategic stability. This is an argument used to perpetuate the possession of nuclear weapons into the indefinite future. China and Russia share this view as well. We need to wage a massive campaign to force the nuclear powers to change their position.

When I recently talked with the representatives of the French Peace Movement and Campaign for Nuclear Disarmament (CND) in Britain, they stated that they would work to pressure their governments to change their stance and ratify the treaty. I pledged solidarity with them, saying that we will work hard as well to urge the Japanese government, which boycotted the U.N. conference and continues turning its back on the convention despite being the government of the world's only A-bombed nation, to depart from the U.S. nuclear umbrella and sign the treaty. This historic convention has given us the united strength to push nuclear states to abandon their nuclear arsenals. Our massive campaign has just started.

In closing, I would like to state proudly that we cannot emphasize enough the role played by the world conference and Hibakusha in opening a new stage for our struggles. The collaboration between national governments and NGOs, which is the form and policy pursued by the world conference, has made a significant contribution to creating the global trend for a nuclear-weapon-free world. In order to carry out our challenging task, let's move forward together with energy and optimism. Thankou.

2, Five major nuclear powers hostile to the Ban Treaty

2018 World Conference against A and H Bombs
August 2, 2018, Hiroshima

As of now, 59 countries have signed and 12 have ratified the historic Treaty on the Prohibition of Nuclear Weapons which was adopted at the UN conference in July 2017. This is significant progress considering the fact that the five major nuclear powers are all hostile to the treaty, claiming that nuclear disarmament should be achieved in a step-by-step manner without undermining strategic stability.

Today's world seems divided over the issue of nuclear weapons. The forces working for the treaty's early entry into force are making progress. On the other hand, the nuclear powers such as the United States and Russia, which had boycotted the UN conference on the treaty, have implemented policies to further enhance for nuclear capabilities.

This May, a heated debate on this issue took place at the second Preparatory Committee for the 2020 NPT Review Conference. The committee is of importance as an international arena for all the parties to the NPT and civil society to meet together and refute the nuclear powers' self-centered claims.

At those opportunities, we will accuse the nuclear powers of enhancing their nuclear capability in breach of Article 6 of the NPT and push them to comply with the article, which requires nuclear-weapon states to "pursue negotiations on a treaty on general and complete disarmament". Focusing on the argument about the humanitarian consequences of the use of nuclear weapons, we will also prove that it is impossible to ensure security by the threat of the use of nuclear weapons. This year's World Conference has great significance as an opportunity for government representatives and anti-nuclear peace movements to exchange views on how to work together to press nuclear-weapon states to abandon their nuclear arsenals.

The most critical element in such discussions is A-bomb survivors' testimonies of living through nuclear hell. Last year, Pope Francis met Masako Wada, Assistant Secretary General of Nihon Hidankyo (Japan Confederation of A- and H-Bomb Sufferers Organizations) and listened to her experience of the A-bomb attack in Nagasaki. After that, the Pope printed and distributed a photo of a little boy standing at a cremation pyre with his dead baby brother on his back, which had been taken by Joe O'Donnell following the bombing of Nagasaki, along with his signature and the caption: "The fruit of war". The Pope has repeatedly sent the message stating, "Nuclear weapons cannot constitute the basis for peaceful coexistence between members of the human family."

Pope Francis, holding a leading position among the 1.2 billion Catholics around the world, also conveyed his message to the UN conference last year and has since expressed his strong support for the nuclear weapon ban treaty. Meanwhile, the Church of England recently welcomed the treaty and called on the British government to "respond positively" to the convention.

In order to urge each country to sign and ratify the nuclear weapon ban treaty, it is crucial to promote the International Signature Campaign in Support of the Appeal of the Hibakusha for the Elimination of Nuclear Weapons. This campaign, called for by nine A-bomb survivors, made a great contribution to the adoption of the landmark treaty. The signature campaign was launched in April 2016, before the nuclear weapon ban treaty came into being. It appealed to all nations around the world to conclude an international treaty to ban and abolish nuclear weapons. Without limiting its purpose to supporting a specific treaty, the campaign wisely, openly, and fundamentally presented a path to achieving an international agreement for the abolition of nuclear arms. Let us expand this signature campaign throughout the world to change the situation proactively.

On June 12, as a historic and global event, the U.S.-North Korea summit was held following the inter-Korean summit in April. The two leaders agreed to build a peace structure and denuclearize the Korean Peninsula. The situation has dramatically changed from last year's height of tension to a resolution through dialogue. This World Conference, having worked to that end, is newly tasked with making continued efforts to promote this process with prospects for peace in Northeast Asia, including the denuclearization of the Korean Peninsula.

Even if there are many twists and turns, the decisive power to bring about peace lies in peoples' movements and public opinion. What has built the new U.S.-North Korea relations is peoples' mounting calls for a resolution not through war but through dialogue.

How things will go also depends on world opinion, as is the case with the issue of eliminating nuclear weapons. Here in Japan, we need to push the Japanese government to sign and ratify the treaty and work to have the North Korea issue resolved through dialogue in the spirit of the war-renouncing Article 9 of the Japanese Constitution.

In June, I took part in an international anti-nuclear meeting in Oxford, England. In these kinds of meetings, I always find - with some exceptions - that civil society's movements are very active in nuclear-weapon states and their allies. In many of the member states of NATO, the majority of the public is in favor of signing the nuclear weapon ban treaty.

In that meeting, I appealed for cooperation for the international signature campaign and discussed the joint efforts to encourage each government to sign the treaty. In Japan, along with the Japanese Communist Party, most opposition parties have come to demand the government's early signature and ratification. Taking responsibility for movements in each country and promoting international cooperation, let us work together to carve out a path to a new era of world peace.

3, Demanding to Conclude a Treaty bans and eliminates nuclear weapons

2016 World Conference against A and H Bombs
August 3, 2016, Hiroshima

February 22nd, 2016 was a historic day. It was the first day of the first session of the U.N. open-ended working group on nuclear disarmament (OEWG) which is looking into the legal steps needed for the elimination of nuclear weapons. In a conference room of the U.N Office at Geneva, the voice of Toshiki Fujimori, Assistant Secretary General of the Japan Confederation of A- and H-Bombs Sufferers Organizations was heard saying, "The only assurance against the risk of using nuclear weapons is the total elimination of nuclear weapons." Following him, on May 4th, Masako Wada, another Assistant Secretary General of the confederation, said, "I call on every state to conclude a treaty which bans and eliminates nuclear weapons." Her appeal was welcomed with a resounding round of applause.

The OEWG which was set up by a U.N. resolution adopted in December 2015 is aimed to "substantively address concrete effective legal measures, legal provisions and norms that will need to be concluded to attain and maintain a world without nuclear weapons." Appeals made by Mr. Fujimori and Ms. Wada there symbolized the new heights of achievements reached by anti-nuclear-weapon movements organized by NGOs and efforts made by governments around the world.

Through the international conferences on the inhumane nature of nuclear weapons which were held three times and the 2015 NPT Review Conference, the majority opinion can be summarized in one sentence: the international community must take legal steps as "effective measures" required by Article VI of the NPT based on deep recognition of the inhumane nature of nuclear weapons. Although the 2015 Review Conference failed to adopt its final documents because of disagreement over the issue of the creation of a WMD-Free Zone in the Middle East, the draft of the final documents reflected the majority opinion to a large degree.

These achievements follow the direction of progress that this world conference has long been calling on the world to make. At last, we are seeing the formal beginning of U.N.-led discussions towards creation of a treaty to eliminate nuclear weapons. What underlies international cooperation and efforts in this regard is the deep awareness of "the inhumane nature of nuclear weapons" which the tragedies of Hiroshima and Nagasaki revealed. Contributions to this newly raised awareness made by this world conference and the testimonies of individual A-bomb sufferers cannot be overstated. The OEWG will submit a report to the U.N. General Assembly this fall.

The political battle map over the issue of elimination of nuclear weapons has become increasingly clearer. 70% of all NPT member states stand for efforts to create a legal framework aiming for the ban and elimination of nuclear weapons by emphasizing the inhumane nature of the weapons. On the other hand, the Permanent Five (P-5) member states which have an exclusive "right" to possess nuclear weapons, namely China, France, Russia, the U.K, and the U.S., are working together to block and suppress the global effort towards elimination of the weapons.

The P-5 states opposed the establishment of the OEWG under the U.N. authority. They argue, "[A] step-by-step approach is the only practical option for making progress towards nuclear disarmament". They also insist, "Addressing further prospects for nuclear disarmament would require taking into account all factors that could affect global strategic stability." This kind of argument means that they just want to postpone the total elimination of nuclear weapons to an indefinite future. In practice, they are against the total abolishment of nuclear weapons.

The P-5 states, which have become very active and unified as a group under the NPT regime since 2009, intimidates governments and anti-nuclear-weapon movements supporting the cause of the OEWG by saying, "[A] ban without the support and participation of the nuclear-weapon states would not eliminate nuclear weapons, but would rather undermine the NPT regime."

Visits to Hiroshima and Nagasaki to deepen the recognition of the inhumane nature of nuclear weapons are of special importance. This is why the visit by U.S president Barak Obama to Hiroshima was welcomed. Yet, some strongly oppose visits to Hiroshima and Nagasaki by world political leaders because they believe Japan was the wartime aggressor and should not be treated as if it were a victim. However, those who lost their lives in the atomic bombings were neither aggressors nor militarist rulers. They were ordinary unarmed civilian men, women and children. Because the use of atomic bombs was unprecedented catastrophe in human history, I believe that it is of great importance for us to urge world leaders to visit Hiroshima and Nagasaki and to ask them to pledge not to allow such catastrophic mistakes to ever be repeated.

The Japanese government abstained from voting for the establishment of the OEWG, but attended the sessions. However, the government just spoke on behalf of the P-5 states and argued "To attain real progress in nuclear disarmament, it is essential to ensure the united actions of the entire community, including the nuclear-weapon states." It also stated, "[We need] a focus on not just humanitarian but also security considerations." It advocates an "incremental approach to nuclear disarmament" which is based on the P-5's "step-by-step approach" and plays the role of blocking constructive discussions at the OEWG. Japan is now acting as if it were the "Trojan Horse" fielded by the P-5 states and is strongly criticized for the shameful role it is playing. We need to politically challenge the Japanese government role with much more criticism to force it to change its stance.

The new security legislation which the Abe government and its ruling coalition enacted by destroying Japan's constitutionalism could lead Japan to even more dependence on the supposed "nuclear umbrella" of the U.S. The Abe administration even argues that Japan's possession of nuclear weapons would not be unconstitutional. This is a very dangerous argument.

In order to make progress towards the total elimination of nuclear weapons by overcoming these hostile obstructions, we must increase more rapidly and strongly public support for a treaty to ban and eliminate nuclear weapons by strenuously conducting international signature campaigns initiated by the Hidankyo and this conference. The need for a strongly invigorated campaign with full public support is especially significant. I renew my commitment to this cause and call on everyone concerned to work together to achieve our aim. Thank you.

4, 70th anniversary of the atomic bombings of in Hiroshima and Nagasaki

2015 World Conference against A and H Bombs
August 3, 2015, Hiroshima

Dear friends,

We convene here today on the occasion of the 70th anniversary of the atomic bombings of in Hiroshima and Nagasaki while Japan's Diet is deliberating the passage of new security bills in its extended session. Japan has two faces which contrast sharply with each other. The one is the Japanese government. The government ought to take on the solemn obligation to lead global efforts to eliminate all nuclear weapons. However, it has blocked the move to create a nuclear weapons convention in order to support U.S. nuclear policy and is attempting to lead the nation again onto a path to participate in wars by imposing new war legislation which thwarts the Constitution and goes against the public will.

The other face, as we can witness here, is the face representing peace in which the majority of Japanese citizens have made great contributions to promoting peace in their united efforts to raise public awareness around the world about the inhumane nature of nuclear weapons and have strongly opposed the war bills being discussed at present in the Diet. We are determined to work together to have this new momentum of the public contribute to the success of this year's conference.

Dear friends,

It was unfortunate that the NPT Review Conference held this year failed to agree on the contents of the final document. Still, the discussions at the conference highlighted the complex dynamics in which an overwhelming majority of nations now stand against the nuclear-weapons states which are being forced to clearly reveal their resistance to establishing a world without nuclear weapons. I strongly believe that this new dimension in international relations reflects the important achievements made through the cooperation between governments and civil societies globally over the past five years.

One of the Review Conference First Committee's memos dated May 8 mentioned for the first time creating a legal framework including a nuclear-weapons-ban treaty within a specified timeframe. It states, "The Conference encourages all states to engage, without delay, within the framework of the United Nations disarmament machinery, in an inclusive process to identify and elaborate the legal provisions required for the achievement and maintenance of a world without nuclear weapons." The legal provisions mentioned above can be enacted through various approaches including by a "stand-alone instrument", which could take the form of a nuclear-weapons-ban treaty or a comprehensive nuclear weapons convention that includes a phased program for the complete elimination of the weapons within a specified timeframe. That is what our movement has demanded for many years in our petition campaigns and this is a remarkable breakthrough.

Anticipating this move, the five nuclear-weapons states jointly made a statement dated April 30 to emphasize the need for "practical steps." It states, "We continue to believe that an incremental, step-by-step approach is the only practical option for making progress towards nuclear disarmament, while upholding global strategic security and stability." According to the statement, the "practical steps" mean full implementation of the New START Treaty between the U.S. and Russia; bringing the CTBT into force; and advancing negotiations on the FMCT as well as Nuclear Weapons Free Zones. However, history clearly shows us that such incremental steps have failed to make significant progress towards the elimination of nuclear weapons.

It is the "step-by-step approach" mentioned above that the nuclear-weapons states insist on as their final bulwark against the imposition of complete nuclear disarmament as their "nuclear deterrence" theory has been discredited. The U.S. government continues to repeat that argument. A U.S. report submitted to the Review Conference this year emphasized the need for a "step-by-step approach" in order to reach an agreement on further nuclear disarmament. Behind the U.S. argument is the U.S. nuclear strategy which states, "The United States would consider the use of nuclear weapons in extreme circumstances to defend the vital interests of the United States or its allies and partners." The strategy is now focused on modernizing its nuclear arsenal over the long-term.

The Russian government updated its military doctrine in December 2014 to strengthen its nuclear arsenal in order to counter the moves being made by the U.S. and NATO. It insists on keeping its right to use nuclear weapons in case of a nuclear or non-nuclear attack on Russia.

Equally troubling, the other nuclear-weapons states aligned their stance with the U.S. approach by signing off on the joint statement at the Review Conference and tried to discourage support for a legally binding process toward the elimination of nuclear weapons. The attempt to maintain nuclear arsenals by insisting on a "step-by-step" approach is being taken by the other nuclear-weapons states as well. Deplorably, none of the five nuclear-weapons states in the joint statement introduced any initiative for complete nuclear disarmament during the conference.

Although the U.S. government advocated an incremental approach at the Review Conference, it failed to provide any convincing logic for it. A U.S. representative just argued that "effective measures" were "not limited to ones that are legally binding." Still, he had to concede, "We can also accept that the final phase in the nuclear disarmament process should be pursued within an agreed legal framework." He acknowledged the need for the ban and elimination of nuclear weapons by treaty though he said it would be in "the final stage" of the process.

Ambassador Taous Feroukhi of Algeria, Chair of the Review Conference, delivered the Draft Final Document May 22. You see the outcome from the debates reflected in the inclusion of phrases such as "legal provisions or other arrangements that contribute to and are required for the achievement and maintenance of a world without nuclear weapons" or "the legal provisions could be established through various approaches including a stand-alone instrument or a framework agreement." As the previous Review Conference five years ago used the term "legal framework", the term "legal provisions" used this time shows substantive progress achieved in the conference which the nuclear-weapons states were not able to block.

Our next challenge is to defeat completely the logic of the "step-by-step" approach which is at present the nuclear-weapons states' trump card in response to an overwhelming majority of global public opinion supporting the enactment of a legal agreement, including a nuclear weapons convention, which will ensure a world without nuclear weapons.

Successive declarations adopted every year at the World Conference against A and H Bombs have contributed to galvanizing anti-nuclear movements among people and governments around the world and encircling the nuclear-weapons states that have insisted on keeping the weapons. I conclude my remarks by emphasizing the need for us to stay on course with perseverance to reach our final destination. Thank you for your attention.

Chapter III

Social Development and socialism

1, Global Financial Crisis and Socialism
-In the light of the world structural change-

International Forum in Southwest Univ.
October 26-27, 2009, Chongqing, China

The global financial crisis started in the U.S. in autumn 2008 has had various impacts on the world. I would like to review the problem in the light of the world structural change. I think three structural changes have taken place in the 20th century. First, the era of capitalism as the only system dominating the world came to an end with the Russia's October Revolution. Since then, the socialist development has gathered volume in terms of the status and weight with the Vietnam's Revolution (1945), the China's Revolution (1949) and Cuba's Revolution (1959) as momentums. Second, in the latter half of the 20th century, the colonial system collapsed and the former client countries came to make up a big group, politically independent from the former colonial powers. Third, the Soviet Union and Eastern European countries dismantled. As a result, the U.S. was regarded as the sole superpower and the argument for "long live capitalism" prevailed around the world. Developments in the international situation in the wake of today's global financial crisis have exposed deep contradictions within capitalism, creating at the same time conditions for expanding the potential of developing countries and the superiority of socialism. So what kind of influence do these developments have on the world structural change?

What Has Global Financial Crisis Brought to World?

Let me point out three aspects, which the global financial crisis has brought to the world:

1, Bankruptcy of neoliberalism
The financial crisis started in the U.S. has shown the bankrupt-

cy of neoliberalism, a policy which the U.S. adopted and imposed on the world. The U.S. has tried to impose U.S.-style neoliberal economic system on the economy of each country and the world as a whole in order for U.S. finance capital to reap big profits, because the monetary economy with rampant speculation does not work by the U.S. alone. Neoliberalism is called as "market fundamentalism," but it was actually an economic system in which the U.S. made hegemonic interventions, making the most of its state power. As a result, weakened manufacturing capacity and the hollowing out of industry undermined the very foundation of U.S. capitalism and deepened poverty and divide between rich and poor in every country. The same applies to Japan. This has driven into opposition the Liberal Democratic Party which has continued to rule Japan for more than half a century, and brought the Democratic Party of Japan into power.

2, Rising power of emerging and developing countries

With the aim of coping with the global economic crisis, the G20 countries have held three financial summit meetings: Washington in November 2008, London in April and Pittsburgh in September 2009, with the participation of Russia and a number of developing countries. They adopted unanimously joint economic measures each time. The Pittsburgh Summit statement declared the G20 as "the premier forum" for international cooperation, marking the end of the G7 era led by major industrial countries. Over a long period, incapability of the G7 or G8 including Russia has been pointed out, in dealing with international economic issues, and now the G20 as an effective forum joined by many developing countries has become indispensable both in name and reality.

Under these circumstances, the G4 called BRICs, which consists of four members of the G20, namely Brazil, Russia, India and China, is working as an important forum. Since Brazilian President Lula da Silva proposed its establishment in June 2007 before the outbreak of the international economic crisis, the G4 leaders have held several ministerial-level meetings. They held the G4 Summit meeting in Russia in June this year, and are going to hold its next Summit in Brazil in 2010. The

G4 represents over 40 % of the world population, 15 % of the global GDP and 40 % of the world foreign currency reserves.

In contrast to the relatively declining U.S. position in the world, newly emerging countries, including G4, have been making remarkable advances. The following G4's statements summarize its viewpoints and demands, which are different from those of developed nations:

First, the emerging and developing economies must have greater voice and representation in international financial institutions; second, heads and executives in those institutions should be appointed through an open and transparent, and merit-based selection process; third, there should be a stable, predictable and more diversified monetary system.

Due to the historical background, international financial institutions have operated with developed nations at the centre. But we now face a new situation in which emerging countries make their demands on advanced countries, a situation born of contradictions between the existing economic order and the recent structural changes in the world. To solve this situation, we must deter economic hegemonism of some big countries and respect all states' economic sovereignty and equality based on fairness.

3, Superiority of Socialism

In the midst of the present economic crisis, a wide range of people have begun to argue about the limits of capitalism, and people across the world increasingly recognize that socialism is the direction world's history is heading for. All over the world including Japan, more and more people are interested in Marxism, as seen in publications or college courses on this subject.

The argument for "victorious capitalism" dominant 20 years ago has subsided, and on the assumption of its bankruptcy active discussions are being carried out about a system beyond capitalism. In a number of countries in Latin America a slogan: "socialism in the 21st century" is advanced and is actually being put into action.

We can also see a growing appreciation among the people in China, Vietnam and other countries about the superiority of socialism. Let me tell you what I feel about China:

(1) China has been more or less under the influence of neoliberalism in the same way as other countries, but the neoliberalist tone of argument has lost steam and appreciation of socialism is on the rise. 2) People's trust in the policies with socialist principles is on the rise in appreciation of the economic and social policies against the negative impacts of global economic crisis. You can find its expression in the system enabling macro control of the economy, a shift from dependence on foreign demand to one depending on domestic demand, and measures to fight poverty and to solve problems in rural areas. 3) Capitalist countries including the U.S. have lost their prestige, while China's presence is being widely felt.

(2) On the occasion of the 60th anniversary of the founding of the People's Republic of China, I answered an interview by a Chinese media as follows: "The Chinese revolution offered China the new development for both the country and society heading for socialism. It also offered the international community an historic chance for working for peace and social progress and for bringing about today's structural change in the world." This was the summary of the points I mentioned above. In fact, if China gives full play to the superiority of socialism and makes advances, it will have a great influence on Asia and the world. If it steps backward, it will be a big blow to the world.

The New Economic Policy Lenin got a try was forced to break off, but the path towards socialism through the market economy, launched in the midst of China's reform and open policies it embarked on 31 years ago, is the path no one has ever walked through. In this economy they have to coexist and compete with the capitalist system. It is also the path towards new economic development. Without following this path, there would not have been the advances and the international status China is now enjoying. On the other hand, this gave rise to contradictions and aberrations. China is required to overcome them in the way towards a new advance.

Furthermore, China has a growing responsibility to demonstrate the superiority of socialism in a number of fields. It is required to go forward by winning support from a wider range of people in the world on such tasks as the prohibition and elimination of nuclear weapons, protection of global environment and preservation of resources.

(3) "Globalization" has been an excuse for justifying neoliberalism, but it is in fact a chance for the socialist movement. Globalization is an inherent phenomenon unavoidable in capitalism, seen in the internationalization of trade, investment and markets expanding beyond borders. Marx and Engels pointed out that the globalization of production and consumption through the development of the world market is a revolutionary role played by capital.

We have to shift the past U.S.-led "globalization" to the new international economic order: one to protect the rights of peoples across the world, and one which people can reap benefits from. Faced with the globalization, the principles of the UN Charter should be at the base of the international relations. Ongoing structural changes in the world will promote peace, social progress and the socialist undertaking, but there would not be any spontaneous advances. Proactive efforts by socialist forces will be decisive in creating history and have a strong impact. In this sense, we are at the important crossroads in history, and bear heavy responsibility.

2, Paying High Regard to Specificity and Internal Logic of Social Development

6th World Socialism Forum by Chinese Academy of Social Sciences
October 16, 2015, Beijing, China

Dear comrades,

I appreciate your kind invitation to me to speak at the 6th World Socialism Forum. The focus of my talk is on how the path of social transformation should be.

Through every phase of social transformation or revolutionary change in any nation, it is absolutely necessary to place importance on the internal logic of social development of each individual country and to respect the cultural and historical specificity unique to that country. It is true that there will be no completely self-reliant way of development for any country in this globalized modern era. No nation can insulate itself from outside influence. Yet, it is unacceptable for external forces to sabotage and manipulate one nation's inherently unique path of social development with the use of various measures including the so-called "soft-power."

Strict compliance with the principles and rules that are intended to govern the modern international community is vitally important in order to advance the international relations of the 21st century in a direction that can promote peace and justice.

Dear comrades,
The Program of the Japanese Communist Party, revised in 2004, clearly states, "[A truly democratic Japan will] champion the international order for peace as defined by the U.N. Charter and oppose any hegemonic attempts to violate or destroy it", and "[A future progressive Japan will] exert efforts to establish peaceful co-existence among countries with different social systems and establish dialogue as well as rela-

tions of co-existence among various civilizations with different values."

I myself have visited more than 100 countries over the years and was given the opportunity to expand my first-hand knowledge about the situations of a variety of nations, the various challenges nations face in their varying social developmental phases, and the various policy measures in place to further progress under country-specific conditions. Though I am a member of an opposition party in Japan, I have had the opportunity to become acquainted with many types of social systems through attending the Summit Meetings of Non-Aligned Nations and their ministerial meetings as an observer over the past ten years as well as the OIC Summit Meetings as a guest.

Just before the Iraq War, I visited Saudi Arabia, Jordan, Iraq, Egypt, Qatar and the UAE with the aim to help to facilitate a political resolution to the threat of war. Fortunately, I shared the common view with the governments I visited for the need for a diplomatic solution and avoidance of war. This shared view was based on the principle for peace embodied in the U.N. Charter.

The War in Iraq led by the U.S. was launched with a false claim about the possession of weapons of mass destruction. This arrogant fabrication led to a global spread of terrorism and it also led to the creation of the later rise of the ISIS which has now created a serious crisis situation which we are all facing.

Moreover, under the rhetoric of "Democratization of the Middle East", the U.S. arrogantly tried to impose its definition of "democracy" on Iraq with reckless disregard for its unique history, religious beliefs, and trajectory of social development. Naturally, it failed in its purported mission and brought about utter social chaos with no favorable outcome in sight. Arab societies strongly opposed such an unjustifiable intervention from the onset, claiming, "Arab societies have the maturity and historical experience that enable them to contribute to our common human civilization, and are, indeed, capable of taking charge of their affairs and reforming their internal conditions." (The Alexandria Statement: March 2004)

The opinion expressed in that statement reflects a true understanding of human history. No one can and should self-righteously impose any specific "value" or "values" on others. The failure of the U.S. clearly indicates that any external interference, whether it is overt or covert, with utter dismissal of a nation's cultural and social specificity is likely to lead to grave and even catastrophic consequences.

Dear comrades,
Through our own interaction with the world, we clearly recognize that it is important for nations to choose their own path to social development without external interference.

Each nation has its own internal logic of social development and its own form and pace defined by its own unique history. This must be fully understood. If a specific type of "value" such as so-called "freedom" or "democracy", which some nations have claimed they have achieved, is arbitrarily imposed on other nations as "a universal value", co-existence among nations will be impossible. We must strictly comply with the principle of non-intervention in the internal affairs of other countries. Peaceful co-existence based on mutual understanding and respect for cultural differences is of high importance.

In this context, Asia has its own important experience of the ASEAN. Southeast Asia is arguably the most diverse region in terms of ethnicity, religion, language and culture. This diverse region successfully established the ASEAN, overcame war and hostility, and now is poised to be integrated as a new regional community by the end of this year. This is because they have respected the sovereignty and cultural specificity of each other and have steadfastly upheld the non-intervention principle.

The ICAPP Beijing Declaration, adopted in 2004, states, "All

Asian countries should choose their own development path and development model in accordance with local conditions", and "We advocate strengthening dialogue among different civilizations, seeking common development through interactions… on the basis of fully respecting each other's historical traditions, cultural differences and diversified development paths." It continues, "Asian political parties…should respect other's choices and practices, respect other's internal and external policies established on the basis of conditions in their respective countries, and refrain from interfering in other's internal affairs."

In addition, I believe that there are some commonly shared values that can be applied to all of us and we can identify through dialogue and respectful co-existence. As the Vienna Declaration, unanimously adopted at the World Conference on Human Rights in 1993, states, all governments, regardless of social regime, have a universally shared responsibility to promote and protect fundamental human rights and to bring about happiness among their respective peoples. That each nation exerts its own national sovereign power according to its unique conditions while protecting fundamental human rights and deepening mutual dialogue should be the world norm.

Obviously, different nations have different courses and different tempos in their social development. When we look at the history of the concept of "people's sovereignty" in which all people are equal under the law, Japan realized this only after the end of World War II, which was a mere 70 years ago. France issued its Déclaration des Droits de l'Homme et du Citoyen in 1789 during the French Revolution 220 years ago. However, when it comes to women's suffrage, both nations implemented this only after the end of World War II. In this way, there are substantial differences in courses and tempos which respective nations have experienced in their social development. We must bear in mind that externally imposing notions of "happiness" or culturally specific values could hamper a nation's unique form and pace of development and even undermine international relations.

Above all, the principles of the U.N. Charter must be upheld. In this regard, we believe that dialogue among different civilizations as well as mutual respect for diversity should be the principle for multilateral cooperation on which all political actions are based; dialogue among civilizations should preserve universally appreciated legacies, enrich commonly shared values and prevent fanaticism and terrorism; the beneficial fruits of civilizations in the world should be enjoyed by all nations and peoples; and we should continue to deepen dialogue and strengthen solidarity based on mutual respect for each other's choice of paths toward social development.

Dear comrades,

As we entered the 21st century, in the wake of ongoing structural changes in international relations, we face global challenges that one country or some countries acting in isolation cannot solve. The key to addressing those challenges is solidarity. Solidarity can be expanded and strengthened by enhancing dialogue and maintaining peaceful co-existence. Today, we are living in an era where governments, local municipalities, political parties, and NGOs can work together globally for peace and social progress together with international organizations and regional communities. This type of cooperative relationship is an inevitable form of cooperation when we address issues in which the very survival of the human race is at stake with the pressing issues of addressing climate change and the need for environmental protection, and the necessity to work together for the elimination of nuclear weapons.

In this regard, the World Conference against Atomic and Hydrogen Bombs, which has been held annually in Japan since 1955, is a good example of global solidarity. This conference is held in Hiroshima and Nagasaki every year with the attendance of a wide variety of representatives from the U.N., national governments, local municipalities, and NGOs, and has developed into a forum which influences international politics and policies in regard to total nuclear disarmament.

I am confident that solidarity based on respect for independent and diverse social development among nations will help to promote peace, justice and social progress.

3, "The Belt and Road Project" and Regional Cooperation

The ICAPP Special Conference on "Rebuilding the Silk Road"
October 14-16, 2015, Beijing, China

Dear Friends,
    First of all, I express my appreciation and respect to the Communist Party of China for hosting this ICAPP special conference on a very timely topic.

    The Belt and Road Project that China has proposed is a joint development plan covering a huge area across nations. It not only reaches out westward from Asia to Europe, but also expands eastward to include the islands in the Pacific with the prospect to even touch upon the Pacific coasts of both North and South America. As the proposed project is an endeavor to jointly build and develop infrastructure on a scale that single country acting alone cannot accomplish, expectations for participation from relevant nations are high.

    To meet its massive funding requirement, it is not sufficient to finance only through existing international institutions such as the World Bank and the Asian Development Bank. In this regard, the Asian Infrastructure Investment Bank (AIIB) is established. Other preparations to create alternative development and investment banks are also being made.

    The impact of the success of such a project will not be limited to the economic domain or to future international development policies. As China forges new bilateral and multilateral relations with all related countries, big or small, developed or developing, through the project, it will offer the exciting prospect of establishing a new type of international cooperation.

We hope the Belt and Road Project will contribute to enhancing mutual interest and mutual trust among all relevant nations and to advancing a fair and democratic international economic and political order.

Businesses in many nations are already preparing to benefit by being included as participants in the proposed plan. In Japan, companies are increasingly engaging in information-gathering and in depth consideration of participation in the project. While many nations have joined the AIIB, the Japanese government refuses to join the bank. We believe Japan should be a member of the bank and play its role in helping to formulate rules for creating a new international finance system that could lead to a new fair and democratic international economic order.

Dear friends,

This project has been proposed and enabled under circumstances where China has achieved great economic development and accordingly raised its political profile in the international arena. China still has a lot of room to grow given the fact that its per capita GDP is 7,589 dollars with a ranking 80th in the world. China's fiscal order is rather robust as its current account balance of payments enjoys a huge surplus with 209 billion dollars in 2014 especially in comparison with the U.S. (with deficit of 410 billion dollars) and Japan (with its slight surplus of 24 billion dollars). Though lack of transparency in the workings of the Chinese economy is discussed, China's economic power can be said to have already reached a point that it greatly influences the world economy particularly since China's current economic situation has entered a new stable growth phase following its past high growth phase.

China's rise is proceeding in parallel with seismic changes in international relations. The global economic power balance has recently changed between North and South (advanced economies and emerging economies) as well as between East and West (Asian countries and Western countries). In 2014, China's GDP based on purchasing power parity became the largest in the world, surpassing that of the U.S. Its GDP on a dollar basis exceeded Japan's in 2010 and became twice that of Japan in 2014.

This ambitious plan—the Belt and Road Project—has been proposed while China's economy is increasingly having a global impact. When a larger power conducts a huge project across its borders, most countries which take partnership with it are usually smaller ones. In this regard, special attention is required to be paid to the following point.

A major power is required to fully understand their partners' positions and sentiments and behave keeping in mind that smaller nations might have some difficulty to expressing their concerns directly even when the principle of equal footing and mutual benefit has been agreed upon. As China itself admits, there are some concerns and skepticism over China's ulterior motives in proposing this project in the first place. It is notable that a Chinese expert has said, "We need to put ourselves in the position of others in advance."

A major leading power is also required to take a careful approach in order for this type of project not to adversely affect the existence of regional mechanisms already in place. This project geographically covers areas where territorial disputes exist and diplomatic solutions are needed. It also covers important sea-lanes for many countries. It is necessary for us to take a very careful approach in order not to complicate existing disputes and problems in proceeding with the project.

In this regard, it is very important that the Chinese government has stated officially in its statement "Vision and Actions", "The Belt and Road cooperation features mutual respect and trust, mutual benefit and win-win cooperation, and mutual learning between civilizations." We need to work together to enable this feature of mutuality to prevail through every phase of the project and advance the project with enhanced mutual trust.

I believe that this is the way to promote "People-to-People Bonds", which is a theme of today's forum, and to mark the beginning of "New

Dialogue between Civilizations."

Dear friends,

Many research institutions in the world have concluded that China will exceed the U.S. economically sooner or later. Some even predict the re-emergence of an era where China's GDP occupies 30-40% of the entire global GDP, which was the reality from the 15th century to the early 19th century.

While the U.S. is not willing to admit to this possibility, an era will come where China replaces the U.S. as the major power in the world. This replacement is anticipated to take place without resorting to wars, which is very different from past trajectories of history. This is in part because both nations realize that war with each other is unacceptable even though they have many contradictory interests.

We hope China will illustrate how a major power in the 21 century should act through the implementation of this project.

China has distinctive features that distinguish it from other major powers which rose in the 19th or 20th centuries.

First, China is rising in an era that can be called the era of the G-193 where the U.N. Charter influences international politics and smaller countries have been enabled to become more important players. In contrast, the U.S. and the U.K. rose in the past through the power struggles involving wars for hegemony among imperialistic powers.

Second, China as a leading country in Asia and Africa has actively engaged in promoting important principles of the modern international politics such as self-determination of peoples or protecting national sovereignty embodied in the Five Principles of Peaceful Coexistence or the Ten Principles of Bandung.

Third, while other past major powers have been imperialistic powers, China espouses socialism.

These are notable distinctions China has compared to the other major powers. I hope the Belt and Road Project, a long-term endeavor, will be successful with China gaining trust and respect globally and that it will bring about peace, harmony and prosperity in the regions involved.

Chapter IV

Environment Preservation, Nuclear disaster & Human Trafficking

1, Experience and Lessons of Japan's Environmental Pollution of the Past 50 Years

The ICAPP Special Conference on *"Promoting Green Development and Building a Beautiful Asia Together"*
May 29-31, 2013, Xi'an, China

Excellencies,
Distinguished delegates,
Ladies and gentlemen,

As a representative of the Japanese Communist Party, I sincerely welcome the ICAPP Special Conference on "Promoting Green Development and Building a Beautiful Asia Together" held in this ancient capital, Xi'an. Environmental issues pose some of the most important questions now faced by every Asian nation on the path of economic development. It is timely to exchange views and learn from each other so that we can be successful both in economic development and in environmental preservation.

In this regard, Japan has gone through bitter experiences for the past 50 years. Although this is far from a mission accomplished, I would like to introduce to you the development of Japan's popular movement to oppose environmental pollution and to protect the public's life and health, and lessons learned from it. Especially, I focus on how citizens fought against the polluting corporations through legal action and changed the attitude of the central and local governments through legislation.

Japan embarked on the policy of economic development with a focus on heavy and chemical industry since the 1950s. In the period of high economic growth in the 1960s and 1970s, serious air and water pollution took place in every corner of Japan. Among the so-called 8 biggest environmental destructions in the world in the 20th century, two occurred in the United States, one each in the UK and Belgium, and the rest, four occurred in Japan.

One of them was Yokkaichi Asthma. In Yokkaichi City in central Japan, massive petrochemical complexes were built since the late 1950s, which produced huge amounts of air pollutants, including sulfur oxide (SOx). Throughout the year, the city was covered by a yellowish smog up to 500 meters high. Because of the bad odor, residents could not even open their windows. Local residents suffered from serious, if not fatal, respiratory disease, which was called "Yokkaichi Asthma." There were more than 6 thousand patients nationwide by 1972 (when the court held 6 polluting companies responsible for the disease in a landmark judgment).

A similar situation was seen in Tokyo. During the winter of 1970 alone, twenty thousand residents in the central district got sick from photochemical smog. At that time, in various industrial districts across Japan, we could not even see nearby buildings.

This environmental destruction was an inevitable result of the nature of capitalism which put profit-making above all else. However, people all across Japan bravely pursued grass-roots movements to preserve clean air, water, and soil, the prerequisite for human survival. In addition, pollution control was greatly advanced by the progressive local governments that spread nationwide at that time with the support of the communists and socialists. The public also fought polluting companies through courts of law. Because the court decisions in these lawsuits more or less acknowledged unlawful behavior by the polluting companies, the firms could not continue operation without instituting anti-pollution measures at various plants. At the same time, the court blamed public administration for inaction. After this, various laws were enacted in the Diet to prevent and mitigate pollution, starting from the Basic Law for Environmental Pollution Control of 1967.

A Diet session in 1970 was dubbed as the "Pollution Diet" where intensive discussion was held on the environmental pollution problem.

One of the most important initiatives made at this Diet session was the deletion of a so-called "economic harmonization" clause from the Basic Law for Environmental Pollution Control that said, "the preservation of environment should be in harmony with the healthy development of the economy." By this, the law was revised in a way that the environment took precedence over economy.

To further restrict air pollution from industrial and other sources, the Air Pollution Control Law (1968) was enacted, followed by introduction of controls on the total amount of sulfur oxide emitted from each designated industrial area in 1974, the first of such pollution control in the world. Emission control of automobiles also advanced with the introduction of the stricter standard on lead and sulfur, as well as nitrogen oxide (NOx).

The struggle towards a better environment never stops. In 1996, a fresh lawsuit started against the automobile industry and public highway corporations to demand stricter emission control of diesel engine vehicles. I was part of this legal action as a Diet member. As for PM2.5 (particulate matter with 2.5μm diameter or less), Japan established an emission standard in 2009. We should have more active countermeasures to control this material which is highly harmful to human health.

Now we can enjoy much cleaner air in Tokyo. A popular way to measure air quality around Tokyo is to count the days we can see Mt. Fuji from Tokyo at the 85-kilometer distance. We can now see Mt. Fuji from Tokyo for approximately 120 days in a year, five times more than we could 50 years ago. This improvement was only possible though a popular struggle to save the public's life and health. This struggle to rein in the greedy nature of capital also helped bring forth in 1978 an emission control law for gasoline vehicles, the strictest in the world (Japanese version of the 1970 U.S. Clean Air Act). The heavy burden imposed by this law on Japanese auto makers in fact spurred them into development of new types of cars with less emission, which eventually became highly competitive in the global market. Summing up, while the strict environmental standards imposed by the public was initially resisted by Japanese capital, this challenge turned out to be a midwife for the cutting-edge technological breakthroughs developed by capital themselves.

Here lies an important message for all of you, my friends. Japan was, and still is, a country where public administration was under the heavy influence of business circles. Because of this, Japan was once a paradise for polluters with the worst environmental records in the world. If this Japan was able to change, then other countries can do a better job of environmental protection before it gets too late with a little bit of political will.

A German environmental expert pointed out lessons from the Japanese experiences, as follows: First, the onus of proof was placed on the polluters; second, environmental information became transparent in a way that the public can have access to it; third, environmental laws were enacted in the Diet, and pollution control agreements were concluded between local governments and businesses; and fourth, innovative technologies were invented to reduce and prevent environmental pollution.

It would be fortunate if the negative example of Japan can prevent others from repeating environmental destruction that Japan experienced in the past. The Japanese public that has endured the serious environmental ordeal is hopeful about establishing a cooperative relationship with other Asian nations to protect our environment.

Friends,
Japan presently faces the most serious environmental destruction caused by the meltdown disaster at the Fukushima Dai-ichi Nuclear Power Plant since March 2011. Because of radioactive contamination, 150,000 residents are still forced to remain in a state of evacuation and not able to return to their hometown. After more than two years have passed, we still cannot identify the causes and mechanism of the meltdown accident nor prevent the leakage of radioactive material from the

destroyed reactors. The most urgent challenge at hand is to tackle the massive amount of radioactively-contaminated water having been used to cool the meltdown fuels, in addition to the underground water continuing to pour into the damaged underground structures of the reactors. TEPCO, operator of the nuclear power plant, and the government are considering the release of the contaminated water into the ocean. However, just after the accident, when Japan released radioactive water into the ocean, it faced the severe criticism from neighboring countries. This act of folly should never be repeated.

Although peaceful use of nuclear energy is a matter of the sovereign right of a nation, I would like to stress that once a severe accident occurs at a nuclear power plant, the ensuing radioactive contamination of air, water, and the soil would be far graver than any past industrial pollution.

Ladies and gentlemen,
In conclusion, I would like to point out that it is indispensable for us to forge regional as well as international cooperation to preserve Asia's environment. This cooperation must base itself on mutual trust and confidence-building. In this respect, the Japanese government's understanding of its past history has often been a hindrance to worldwide cooperation. This problem is getting more and more serious nowadays.

The Japanese government once admitted its "mistaken national policy" in pursuing "its colonial rule and aggression." While this admission itself was not straightforward enough to squarely come to terms with its past, the present government even backtracked on this past statement by asserting that "the definition of aggression has yet to be established academically and internationally. It differs depending on which side you are viewing from." This is tantamount to negating the present international order based on the United Nations Charter. This kind of remark could deprive Japan of its eligibility as a member of international society. It is more than natural that the neighboring countries including the U.S. harshly criticized Japan.

We will do our utmost not only to enhance cooperation to protect Asia's environment, but also to put an end to this toxic contamination of the international political environment.

Thank you for your attention.

2, For enhanced international cooperation in disaster response

ICAPP Special Conference on Natural Disasters & Environmental Protection
March 2-4, 2015, Putrajaya, Malaysia

Mr. Chairman and dear friends,
 I wholeheartedly welcome this international meeting here in Putrajaya.
 I myself had opportunities to visit here twice in the past. The first was in 1999 when the city was still under construction. The second visit was in 2003 when I attended the OIC Summit as a guest, which, I remember, was the first international conference held in Putrajaya.

 Today's topic, disaster response, is very important and timely and it is my honor to be here with you.

 In January, I visited Chile, an earthquake-prone country like Japan. There, a party official told me, "Japan and Chile have several things volcanoes, hot springs, earthquakes, and tsunami. They are all created by God, but we can effectively deal with natural disasters with our own human power." I could not agree more with that remark.

 Since Japan is a country that experiences frequent natural disasters, the nation has a lot of experience with them and has become adept at effective preparation, rapid responses and swift reconstruction.

 Globally speaking, we have witnessed a series of natural disasters. We had earthquakes and tsunami not only in Japan and Chile but also in Sumatra, Indonesia, which is also part of the Ring of Fire. Flood, drought and typhoon disasters are among some other examples those nations had to face. Every time we have a disaster, lives are lost, properties destroyed, sanitation deteriorates and these most negatively impacted are always the poorest sectors of society. Natural disasters could have long-lasting adverse impacts on societies and their economic development unless rapidly responded to and effectively addressed.

Although natural disasters are due to Mother Nature, we are able to prepare for possible disasters in order to minimize damages when they occur, by making full use of advanced science and technology. We can invest more not only in hardware but also in software, such as scheduling disaster drills and paying attention to human resources development to ensure disaster damage prevention.

My firm belief is that it is essential for the Asian community to enhance practical cooperation on a regional scale to prevent and also deal effectively with damages caused by natural disasters. I have advocated that for years.

The ASEAN nations are already cooperating and are expanding the cooperation as they prepare for a new begging as an ASEAN Community this year. There is, however, very little prospect of cooperation on a broader East Asian scale, at least in the near-term. One of the biggest problems here is lack of dialogue and mutual trust among nations in the region. In peace and security issues, it will take longer to forge regional rules and norms to prevent emerging potential conflicts from escalating. But, in this area, the disaster relief issue, everyone feels an urgent need to do something more immediately effective, and thus this can be a starting point from which we can work together to initiate concrete and effective cooperation step by step in a realistic manner. I think it is incumbent upon us to do so.

As far as peace and security is concerned, we have proposed the creation of regional framework for peace and cooperation in North-East Asia, which follows the ASEAN's example of establishing regional rules and norms, including the renunciation of the use of force, promotion of dialogue, and solution of disputes in a peaceful manner so that we can finally have a North-East Asian version of the ASEAN treaty of amity and cooperation. I strongly believe that promoting regional cooperation in disaster relief could significantly contribute to promoting peace and cooperation on a broader Asian scale.

Dear friends,

Nearly 4 years have passed since the great earthquake hit the eastern part of Japan. More than 15,700 lives were officially lost and around 4,500 are still missing. I would like to take this opportunity to express our deep appreciation for the generous support offered to Japan by governments and peoples in Asia following that disaster.

From our experience, one of the most important principles to follow in reconstruction efforts following such a disaster is effective governmental assistance to everyone affected so that they can get back on their feet and restart their lives and businesses. In particular, public financial assistance for reconstruction of houses is crucial because housing is an important part of the foundation of people's lives. Twenty years ago, we had another major earthquake in the Hanshin-Awaji area, which is in the western part of Japan. After the earthquake, the affected local residents made a great effort in pushing lawmakers to create a new law under which the government provides three million yen to help each family reconstruct its totally destroyed house. We are at present demanding that the financial assistance be increased to 5 million yen for each family in order to meet the needs of the disaster-stricken people as well as to expand the assistance to reconstruction not only for totally destroyed houses but also for partially destroyed houses.

Now, even four years after the East Japan Earthquake, 270,000 people are still displaced from their homes and more than 100,000 have been forced to live in temporary housing. More than 3,000 people have died under such difficult living conditions.

When it comes to disaster damage prevention, it is increasingly important for us to transform cities, towns and villages into more disaster-resilient ones. In an earthquake-prone country like Japan, you need to have all important buildings such as schools, hospitals and nursing care facilities inspected and enhanced to be quake-resistant. It is urgent to improve disaster-relief planning to ensure the safety of the elderly, the physically-challenged, and all the local residents.

In addition to that, effective disaster drills are essential. Those make a great difference. In the East Japan Earthquake four years ago, areas where residents had conducted regular disaster drills were more likely to avoid loss of lives due to tsunami than areas where they had not been conducted. "When you see tsunami coming, run up to any place higher!" was the instruction given at an elementary school. So the children ran to the high ground and the adults followed the children, and potentially lost lives were saved. The disaster drills are very helpful and economically practical.

Dear friends,

The East Japan Earthquake had another special aspect of disaster due to the nuclear power reactor meltdown of the Fukushima No.1 plant caused in part by the tsunami. In the ensuing struggle to contain the spread of radioactivity, we have come to the bitter realization of the unique nature of nuclear accidents compared to natural disasters. Once highly radioactive material is released by accident, its impact could be almost limitless spatially and may persist indefinitely because we do not have the technological expertise to fully contain it. This is a very serious problem that could endanger all of humanity.

What is happening there is very serious despite the government's empty assurances that the contaminated water is fully under control. Substantial leakage of the contaminated water to the ocean still continues and the government is very irresponsible as it behaves as if letting the water flow into the ocean were the ultimate solution.

In the Fukushima nuclear plant accident, the amount of exposed cesium, which is a radioactive element, is estimated to be 168 times more than that of the atomic bomb the US dropped on in Hiroshima seventy years ago. 120,000 people who once lived in areas adjacent to the plant site have been displaced. Decontamination work has been slowed due to technical difficulties while cleanup costs have been mounting.

The accident has dealt a serious blow to the livelihood, education, health, welfare and occupational opportunity of the entire local community. Anxiety over food safety and the possible risk of thyroid cancer among children has been spreading in the local community.

The government did not release information about the flow spread of exposed radiation which was detected by a special system called SPEEDI [System for Prediction of Environmental Emergency Dose Information] until 2 weeks after the accident. As the government withheld the information from the public, the local residents were not able to know where radiation levels were high. Actually, people evacuated in the same direction along which the radiation moved, resulting in more exposure to more people.

I think it is necessary that the Japanese government make public its interim assessment on the whole picture of the losses and damages caused by the nuclear reactor accident as well as its review of the effectiveness of measures the government took so that other nations can learn lessons from Japan's experience. Driven by this bitter experience, a majority of Japanese people now is supporting an idea that Japan phase out nuclear power generation and shift immediately to renewal sources of energy. Actually, all nuclear reactors in Japan have been offline since the Fukushima meltdown and, thus, Japanese people have come to realize that they can live without nuclear power.

What I described is our four-year experience and there is little prospect that our struggle against radiation exposure will be over soon. I know, of course, that there is an argument that the peaceful use of nuclear power is the right of every nation and that nuclear power is one way to ensure the diversification of energy sources. As far as Japan is concerned, the country has consistently pushed for nuclear power generation based on the so-called safety myth, claiming nuclear power is a clean energy. But, frankly speaking, the safety of nuclear power generation has long been called into question. In particular, there is no ultimate solution to the nuclear waste problem, which is a serious downside people derisively refer to "a house without a toilet".

Although natural disasters continue to happen, you can prepare for them and minimize possible damages. But a nuclear power accident is extremely difficult to contain and adequately prepare for.

Each nation has a right to decide its own energy policy. I have reported today on the difficulties we are facing in Japan, hoping to draw your attention to the consequences we now face due to political inertia.

Finally, I wish this meeting a great success as an important opportunity to promote further cooperation in disaster damage prevention and effective reconstruction efforts in Asia. Thank you for your attention.

3, Human Trafficking Today

3rd ICAPP Workshop on Human Trafficking
March 12, 2016, Islamabad, Pakistan

Honorable chairperson,
Distinguished delegates,
Ladies and Gentlemen,

Thank you for giving me this opportunity to discuss the topic of human trafficking today, and I appreciate the initiative taken by the ICAPP Workshop on this serious issue. And allow me to express my sincere gratitude to Pakistani political parties for hosting the 3rd Workshop.

We have great interest in sharing each other's knowledge and experiences on this global issue toward our shared goal to eliminate human trafficking and ensure that human dignity and fundamental human rights are protected in our regions and throughout world.

Japan is a country where sexual exploitation of women and children, Japanese and foreign, and labor exploitation of foreigners, both men and women, is rampant. Japan is a destination, source, and transit country in human trafficking with one of the worst records among major developed countries.

Japan has faced sharp criticism as it "does not fully comply with the minimum standards for the elimination of trafficking" (Trafficking in Persons Report by the U.S Department of State). The Modern Slavery Index issued by the Walk Free Foundation in 2014 shows that Japan ranks 22nd in the number of "modern slaves" among 167 countries. However, efforts to raise public awareness on the issue by media and others concerned have been inadequate in regard to the seriousness of the matter that the human trafficking issue has become a "hidden social problem" in the nation.

Today, I would like to bring up the problem of sexual exploitation in the sex industry and illegal businesses and the situation of labor exploitation of foreigners in the "Technical Intern Training Program" run by the government.

Sexual exploitation in Japan has grown along with the commercialization of sex as seen in the huge sex industry and amounts of readily available pornography.

With more than 30,000-registered sex related businesses and more than 100,000 estimated workers, the sex industry runs openly in Japan. As an inevitable result, this industry, in combination with organized crime and illegal businesses, has become fertile soil for human trafficking of foreign and Japanese women and children who are exploited by means of threat or use of force, or other forms of coercion, of fraud, and abuse of power associated with their positions of vulnerability.

We have found a number of cases that constitute grave offences to human dignity and fundamental human rights. International organizations such as the International Labor Organization, NGOs and media reveal that brutal and totally unacceptable crimes occur in Japan which is supposedly governed under the rule of law with the Anti- Prostitution Law which was enacted in 1956 and the Convention on the Elimination of All Forms of Discrimination Against Women ratified in 1985.

Let me cite an example from media reports: a 16-year-old high school student was forced to work as a sex slave for years after she was raped in a town and her personal data was stolen from her student ID and mobile phone. Just before entering her senior year in high school, her desperate bid to escape from the sex work was accepted by the "organization", seemingly because the organization had other high school girls like her to take her place. However, even after quitting, she had to continue to work in the sex industry in order to pay the exorbitant amount of money demanded by the organization to delete her pornographic videos that had been uploaded to the Internet.

NGOs have also found many cases which indicate that Japanese women were victimized by tricks used by recruiters so that women believed they would work as "fashion models" or "actresses". But in reality they were threatened and forced to be in porno movies usually under false contracts. These heinous acts are conducted against the backdrop of the existence of the approximately 400-million-dollar porno industry and the flood of child pornography available in Japan.

Human trafficking beyond national borders has been grave as well. Foreign victims of human trafficking in Japan are mainly from developing countries in Asia. They are recruited as migrant workers, but after arriving in Japan, they become aware that they are under a huge amount of debt and are put under many forms of threat or coercion, and are then forced to work in prostitution or sex industry.

The Japanese NGO Lighthouse estimates there are more than 54,000 Japanese and foreign victims of sexual exploitation in Japan. Walk Free estimates there is 240,000 modern slaves in our country including victims of sexual exploitation. The actual extent of suffering is so grave that it is hard to imagine.

Under the current laws of Japan, those acts may constitute crimes of rape, child pornography, blackmail or others, but may not be prosecuted under the crime of human trafficking due to the narrow legal definition of "human trafficking" which punishes only for the buying and selling of a person. The police officially confirmed only 44 cases of human trafficking in 2015.

Friends,
In regard to the human trafficking issue, I would like to take this opportunity to touch upon a serious historical issue related with the matter. That is the so-called "comfort women" issue. Some of you here might wonder why the "comfort women" issue caused by the Imperial Army of Japan during WWII still matters even now, more than 15 years

into the 21st century.

This grave issue is a very contemporary matter as the issue of modern human trafficking is highlighting the ignorance of the 20th century's achievements in promoting fundamental human rights and the right to dignity of women and all people.

I have addressed the "comfort women" issue as Chairperson of the International Commission of the JCP as well as a Member of the House of Councilors of Japan for years after I first heard the serious accusations related to the matter raised by members of Korean NGOs at a conference of the former United Nations Commission on Human Rights in Geneva in 1992.

The core of the "comfort women" issue is institutional and systematic exploitation of women and utter denial of their dignity by the Japanese military, or the state-power of Japan. As the 1993 statement issued by Chief Cabinet Secretary Yohei Kono admitted, "comfort women" were women and girls who were taken to the "comfort stations" which were built and managed, directly or indirectly, by the Army and held in custody to be forced to serve as sex slaves.

Some Japanese politicians and even cabinet members who want to whitewash Japan's heinous wartime policy and its responsibility have been arguing over the definition of "coercion" in order to deny the coercive nature of the matter. The Government of Japan was unwilling to apologize to or compensate the victims. This attitude of the Japanese government is once again a denial of the right to dignity of the victims, an obstacle in the way of the international efforts to promote human rights and eliminate human trafficking, and what has left the "comfort women" issue still unresolved even today.

Recently, Japan and the Republic of Korea agreed to a "settlement" of the issue. While the bilateral relations between both nations which deteriorated due to the Abe administration's inflexibility has been improved by the "settlement", there is a long way to go for all former "comfort women" to feel that their honor and dignity have been fully restored.

Despite the fact that Japan, as offender, is responsible to implement the "settlement", a Japanese official denied in effect the core point of the 1993 Kono Statement by saying at a recent U.N. meeting that the government could not find out any evidence of coercive transportation of women by military personnel or authorities. The coercive nature in this matter has been widely accepted in the international community and recognized even in court rulings in Japan. The denial of this core point by the government strongly indicates its lack of sincerity to honor the full implementation of the "settlement". It also raises doubts over Japan's determination to protect women and all people from sexual exploitation and human trafficking, a modern form of slavery.

On March 7th, the U.N. Committee on the Elimination of Discrimination against Women (CEDAW) pointed out in its concluding observations on Japan's seventh and eighth periodic reports: "The issue of 'comfort women' gives rise to serious violations that have a continuing effect on the rights of victims and survivors of those violations that were perpetrated by the state party's military ". The committee called on Japanese leaders and public officials to "desist from making disparaging statements" regarding the former "comfort women" and urged the Japanese government to "recognize the right of victims to a remedy and accordingly provide full and effective redress and reparation".

As this issue is directly linked to Japan's war crimes, I would like to emphasize that the issue will be never resolved unless the Government of Japan shows sincere remorse for its actions during the war.

Friends,
In addition to sexual exploitation, the forced labor problem is another form of human trafficking that exists in Japan. In particular, the government's Technical Intern Training Program (TITP) that was intro-

duced in 1993 has provided a loophole in the Labor Standard Acts which has led to rampant forced labor in Japan as a result.

Under the name of "internship", migrant workers from Asian countries work under forced labor conditions in factories or farms. In some cases, they are forced to work even over 20 hours per day or without days off for very low pay far below the minimum wage. A journalist reported that one factory in the central part of Japan fines "technical interns" for going to the toilet in order to keep them working at the production line.

It is not rare that employers take measures to prevent foreign workers from escaping or communicating with people outside by the use of an automatic wage deposit system at the company or by confiscating interns' passports. Worse, sexual harassment and violence against interns also occurs due to their positions of vulnerability.

There are 170,000 foreign "technical interns" nationwide, many of whom are de facto migrant workers (2014). Most of them are from other East Asian countries which have become a major source of cheap workers without rights in Japan with its shrinking native labor force. The number of missing interns who escaped from their hosts amounts to approximately 5,000 annually (the Ministry of Justice, 2015).

Although labor authorities have not effectively monitored and regulated the program, it still found that 76% (2,977/3,918) of the host organizations violated the Labor Standard Act last year.

This is nothing less than de facto labor slavery approved by the law-based institution which was originally intended to "help young people in developing courtiers learn technical skills".

Friends,
Human trafficking is a global challenge that needs to be overcome and it is crystal clear that international cooperation among various par-

ties concerned is vital. Effective cooperation among nations which are source and destination countries is also essential in order to implement appropriate protection of these workers against human rights violations. Sharing information in regard to the real situation of workers and enhancing collaboration to prevent forced labor and human trafficking in any form are especially helpful.

At the same time, I would like to emphasize the urgent need of enhanced efforts by Japan itself in order to eliminate the violation of universal human rights through both sexual and labor exploitation.

The Government of Japan has made some efforts to tackle the human trafficking problem by developing a national plan of action, setting up a governmental committee for combating trafficking in humans, amending laws on immigration, and criminalizing the buying and selling persons. However, the government has yet to fulfill its responsibility to meeting with the minimum standards for the elimination of trafficking.

Pushed by the widespread criticism on the Intern Training Program, the Government submitted a reform bill which includes measures to strengthen the monitoring of and control over the program. However, at the same time, without a fundamental review of the program, the bill allows the expansion of the scale of the program and the total number of interns involved, period under contract and jobs available in response to requests from employers.

As we touched upon some cases of human trafficking committed in Japan, we can clearly recognize the need for comprehensive actions ranging from strengthening law enforcement, combating organized crime, regulating illicit industries, narrowing income gaps, eliminating poverty (in both developing and developed countries), enhancing public awareness of human rights, especially of women and children, and promoting a healthy, just, progressive society and culture. The government has primary responsibility to take comprehensive actions to that end.

In conclusion, I would like to highlight the importance of raising public awareness and promoting collaboration with civil societies. In a survey taken in Japan in 2012 by Lighthouse, it was found that 81.3% of respondents were not aware that Japanese are victims of human trafficking inside Japan. We need to increase people's awareness drastically in order to increase public participation in and support for comprehensive actions to combat human trafficking, especially at the civil society level. As I mentioned above, civil societies and NGOs have been playing leading roles in this effort ahead of governments. We believe that cooperation and collaboration between political parties and civil society will enhance our capacity to tackle the challenges. And we will make every effort to fulfill our responsibility to protecting the human dignity of all.

Thank you for your kind attention.

Chapter V

Mahatma Gandhi & Social Development

Mahatma Gandhi and Japan
-An Approach towards East Asian Peace-

The International Conference on Gandhi, Disarmament and Development
October 4-6, 2013, Indore, Madhya Pradesh, India

Honorable chairperson,
Distinguished delegates,
Ladies and Gentlemen,

I heartily welcome the convening of the International Conference on Gandhi, Disarmament and Development on the heels of October 2, Gandhi Jayanti, which is also commemorated as the International Non-violent Day by a decision of the United Nations General Assembly.

A, Gandhiji and Japan

Mohandas Karamchand Gandhi has been the subject of extensive studies by many scholars in India and the world. Among the voluminous literature on Gandhiji, I would like to introduce a work by a Japanese, a contemporary of Gandhiji, who studied him. This will show you how Japan and India are deeply related to each other.

His name was YOHENA Chitaro (1891-1960). A journalist and an editor, he had a keen interest in Korea under Japan's colonial rule as well as India long under the British Raj. At the same time, he took an increasingly critical position against imperialism and capitalism.

In 1922, he published two books, namely "Gandhi and Satyagraha"(Ganji to Sinri no Haji) and "Gandhi's Judgment Day"(Ganji Simban no Hi). Although there was very limited interest in India and Gandhi at that time in Japan, he took up Gandhi's thoughts as a leader of the Indian national movement, arguing that the people of India were behind his leadership.

Yohena closely followed the move toward independence for India, a gigantic political transformation which helped Yohenha develop his ideas on anti-imperialism, national independence, and people's movements into a coherent theoretical system. What he especially paid attention to was the core idea of Gandhiji's philosophy, "satyagraha" -- non-violent resistance.

Born in Okinawa, which was occupied by the U.S. military in the closing days of WWII in 1945, Yohena was inspired by Gandhi's thinking to participate in the Okinawan people's movement. In November 1945, he founded the Okinawajin Renmei (Okinawan Federation) and later spearheaded the mobilization that demanded Okinawa's reversion to Japan.[9]

Back in the days of Japan's militarist rule, however, even to write about Gandhi's effort for national independence was severely restricted. Despite such difficulties, he courageously argued for the independence of Korea, as he applied Gandhi's thought to Korea.

Gandhiji was assassinated by a Hindu nationalist in 1948, just after India's independence. However, Gandhiji's thought and movement was inherited by Jawaharlal Nehru, who laid the foundation for India's democracy and nation building.

As regards India's relationship with Japan, the government of India led by Nehru did not attend the San Francisco Peace Conference promoted by the U.S., but concluded a peace treaty of its own with Japan in 1952. Nehru was said to have concluded the treaty out of his desire that Japan regain her honor, freedom, and equality with other nations.

---

[9] "Yohena Chitaro : Between Okinawa and India" (in Japanese) by Heiji Nakamura (presently professor emeritus of the Tokyo University of Foreign Studies)

Now we are in 21st Century facing with a different set of tasks than those of Gandhiji's era. Nevertheless it is still highly significant for us to carry on his efforts towards peace, national independence and social progress. This is why we should remember Gandhiji in the present world.

B, Present-day world and Japan

The 20th century began with global domination by monopoly capitalism and imperialism. During the last century, however, great changes took place, such as the collapse of colonialism, and establishment of the right of national self-determination as a recognized international principle. We are also free from the shackles of the Cold War which forced many countries to choose to join either the U.S. camp or the Soviet camp. Even though there remain imperialism, hegemonism, and outrageous behavior carried out on their behalf, we live in an era when the right to national self-determination and the right to development are accepted as the main pillars of the international human rights guarantee in which every country is able to pursue the development path it freely chooses.

In recent years, developing and emerging countries have increased their weight in the global economy. Those countries are able to tackle various international issues without being constrained by the great powers' beck and call. Now is the time when they are collectively moving the world. Take for example international decision-making in the economic field: developed capitalist countries are no longer able to deal with any problems by themselves without having developing countries on board.

Moreover, this is not the age when a military alliance between countries can be a mainstay of a country's diplomatic strategy. By getting rid of military alliances, Southeast Asia and Latin America have made great strides in ensuring security through confidence-building and dialogue without assuming imaginary enemies.

Look at East Asia, widely regarded as a region of high growth and rapid development with its amount of trade and investment exceeding half of the world total. India and China have increased clout both politically and economically. In this region with significant market and political influence, Japan should be playing its due role. Unfortunately, Japan is still tied down by its military alliance with the U.S. with the massive presence of U.S. military bases. Diplomatically as well as politically, Japan is left far behind by the rest of the world and other Asian countries that are pursuing independent diplomacy.

In order to build peace in East Asia, the JCP attach great importance to Japan's diplomacy based on the pacifist spirit enshrined in the preamble and Article 9 of the Constitution. We are making our utmost effort to prevent Japan from becoming a country that would join wars along with the U.S.

We are advocating for abrogation of the Japan-U.S. Security Treaty, which has been the source of Japan's aberrant subordination to the U.S. Our vision is that Japan conclude with the U.S. a friendship treaty, turning the lord-vassal relationship into a true friendship between equals. A new Japan will not take part in any military alliances and seek to join a path of peace, neutrality so that Japan can have friendly ties with all the countries in the world. I have been attending several summit meetings of the Non-Aligned Movement as a member of an NGO delegation with the observer status. It is my ardent hope that Japan become a member of this movement in the future.

Removal of the U.S. military bases in Japan is an uphill task. Even though Okinawa returned to Japan in 1972, as was desired by Yohena, the U.S. base situation has not changed since under the direct U.S. military rule. Although the area of Okinawa is just 0.6% of Japan, 75% of the U.S. bases in Japan are concentrated in Okinawa. The massive presence of the U.S. military bases, which occupy 18% of total area of Okinawa, and the U.S. troops constitute a threat to the lives of the residences and an obstacle to healthy development of the local economy.

In Tokyo, we have huge Yokota Air Base. In its vicinity, Yokosuka Naval Base, a mother port of one of the aircraft carriers of the Seventh Fleet also exists. No foreign military bases are ever located in the midst of such densely populated areas. This situation is out of touch with the present global trend.

In Japan today, a hotly debated issue is Japan's participation in the negotiations of the Trans Pacific Partnership agreement (TTP). This U.S.-led agreement is basically aimed at total abolition of tariffs. It also includes trade liberalization of agricultural products, privatization of postal service, and liberalization of finance and insurance which have been demanded by the U.S. Joining the TPP would deprive Japan of its policy independence in finance, foreign exchange, commerce, and agriculture, totally transforming the way Japan is today by imposing the "American way." We oppose joining the TPP and strive for equitable and mutually beneficial economic relationship with all the nations.

C, Towards a world without nuclear weapons

In conclusion, I would like to speak on elimination of nuclear weapons, a goal that all human beings aspire for. I am a co-chairperson of the World Conference against A&H Bombs, which is held annually in August in Hiroshima and Nagasaki, the two cities on which atom bombs were dropped respectively on 6th and 9th August 1945. I appreciate that Indian delegations attend this conference every year.

Here I recall a famous quote by Gandhiji.

> "The atomic bomb has deadened the finest feelings that sustained mankind for ages. (...) The atom bomb brought an empty victory to the Allied armies, but it resulted for the time being in destroying the soul of Japan. What has happened to the soul of the destroying nation is yet too early to see."

Is fact, the atomic bombing still torments the living survivors and its after-effects are felt in the second and third generations even after 68 years.

This year's World Conference held in August focused cruelty and inhumanity of nuclear weapons and solemnly declared that human beings cannot coexist with nuclear weapons and that abolition of nuclear weapons is a vitally important goal on which human survival depends. It also called for all-out efforts to create an overwhelming joint action of people worldwide towards early commencement of negotiations of a Nuclear Weapon Convention.

68 years since Gandhiji deplored the use of nuclear weapons and worried about the future course of the human society, human beings have certainly imparted their wisdom and made progress by creating a powerful movement that elucidates the way to eliminate this malicious human creation, namely nuclear weapons. Thank you for your attention.

英語　緒方靖夫国際問題演説集

2019年10月15日
著者　緒方靖夫
発売　ジャパン・プレス・サービス
〒151-0051　東京都渋谷区千駄ヶ谷4-25-6
　電話：03-3423-2381
　ファクス：03-3423-2383
電子メール：info@japan-press.co.jp
印刷・製本：株式会社 光陽メディア

＊落丁、乱丁がありましたらお取り替えいたします。
ISBN 978-4-88048-093-0